LOVE'S DANCE

–The Catboat of the Caymanes

*"And the skill in sailing them, that should be preserved.
That is an art."–Captain Paul Hurlston, Master Mariner*

CAYMAN MARINER SERIES

**Stories and Photography of the
Caymanian Catboat**
Compiled and edited by H.E. Ross
Sponsored by the Cayman Islands Seafarers' Association

ISBN 1-930313-00-4

COPYRIGHT © 1999

BY H.E.ROSS

DESIGNED BY THE GRAPHIC OVERFLOW

PRINTED BY MASTER LITHO INC.

TABLE OF CONTENTS

FOREWORD

By Walsham R. Connolly, JP
President,
Cayman Islands Seafarers' Association

The Cayman Islands Seafarers' Association is a not-for-profit organization, committed to preserving and promoting an awareness of the maritime heritage of the Cayman Islands. Our objectives contribute to the educational, economic, cultural and social enrichment of these Islands.

We have started to work toward these objectives, and the level of support given by the community and those who respect our culture is determining the degree of our success. The objectives of the Association include a comprehensive history of the seafaring tradition of the Cayman Islands, emphasising the importance of the maritime industry to the cultural and socio-economic development of these Islands, as well as the raising and investing of funds to finance the objectives of the Association.

The photographic essay, *LOVE'S DANCE-The Catboat of The Caymans*, is an effort to emphasise a foundation in our overall history, the Catboat. We of the Islands have made a large part of our maritime heritage incidental to our present cultural development.

We are changing this now. The Cayman Islands Seafarers' Association is initiating a series of maritime historical books, beginning a maritime library and museum, promoting maritime training and careers. We feel that we owe our oncoming generations an overall, comprehensive historical foundation and we feel it our duty to address the nautical cornerstone of that foundation.

The Caymanian Catboat was the mainstay in transportation amongst our Islands, as well as serving as a pivotal means of employment for most of our history. The Cayman Islands Seafarers' Association invites you to look at the development of the Caymanian Catboat in these pages and to share our pride in being one of the foremost seafaring nations in the world. It has been our repute to be the best and that nautical heritage belongs to all Caymanians.

The Lydia E. Wilson/CINA

ACKNOWLEDGEMENTS

A list of acknowledgements of those who have assisted in this project cannot be complete, so I will note only those whose direct and unfailing support produced *LOVE'S DANCE*. First, outside the Caymans, where the project began, I wish to give absolute thanks to Susan Schiele for her strength of encouragement and faith; to Bob Bonnet, who loaned me the boat, time and money to get here and get started; to Kate Hegre for her cheerful certitude; my children, Ian and Maya; to Sara Ross and the memory of Jana Ross; Lucy Mott for being Lucy; to Liz and Tom Davidson; Lynn; Josh Pryor; my friend, David Caissie and son Dante; the great photographer, David Major; the San Francisco poet-laureate, Lawrence Ferlinghetti.

In the Caymans, I am grateful to Captain Marvin Ebanks and the guys at Captain Marvin's Watersports; to Rollin and Christine Jackson, who gave me an office at Tropicana Tours with telephone, Fax and transportation, and believed in the importance of *LOVE'S DANCE* to the culture of the Cayman Islands; to Ronnie, Ruth, Helene and Lucas for making me a family member; to Anita, Suzie and Bill at the CI National Museum for pointers; to Tammy, Heather, Annabelle, Craig, Duncan, Jan and Dr. Philip Pedley at the CI National Archive, without whom research for a book of this sort would take years; to the whole of the CI Seafarers' Association, a repository of knowledge and wisdom; especially to photographer Valerie Cottier.

I dedicate *LOVE'S DANCE* to the spirit and memory of my friend Captain Ernest Maggio.

H.E. Ross,
Editor

Pulling Turtle Into A Catboat/CINA

Getting a Haircut/CINA

On Deck,
Lydia B. Wilson/
CINA

INTRODUCTION

"They were the everlasting children of the mysterious sea. Their successors are the grown-up children of a discontented earth."

– Joseph Conrad

The Caymanian Catboat is linked closer to the development and history of the Cayman Islands than any other single entity outside religion, the turtle and the geophysics of the place itself. Every person living upon the three oceanic mountain rims, up until the cultural ascendancy of the tourism and banking industries, has been somehow affected by the use of these rakishly graceful vessels. So integral a part was the Catboat in daily life that its demise was not noticed in much the way that something once precious can be taken for granted.

In a strange prioritive, the little Sunfish® sailing boat, representing a concept of tourism, is featured on the Cayman Islands' five-dollar bill. The Caymanian Catboat, however, which has evolved with these Islands, is not displayed in currency but is featured on seven stamps issued between 1935 and 1980. And almost every Islander has an affectionate Catboat story. These numerous stories are the reason for the creation of LOVE'S DANCE-The Catboat of the Caymans as the initial publication in a Cayman Mariner series.

LOVE'S DANCE seeks to describe a strong, gentle and graceful people who view common sense as an art form, and who have manifested that art form in the Caymanian Catboat. Caymanians, for most of their history, have risked their lives and the livelihoods of their families upon the passed on and accumulated wisdom and knowledge of the vagaries of the sea. The Catboat is the result of their collective striving for perfection in a love's dance upon the horizon of the practical and the romantic.

The Caymanians who have written the following pages were and are conscious of the phenomenal material affluence that has, relatively rapidly, come into their communities. They have committed themselves to paper with an intention to stimulate the preservation and evolution of their seafaring heritage. It is not difficult to draw a corollary between the development of the Catboat and that of the Caymanian.

In these pages we explore the Caymanian Catboat origins, its development and manifestations, its sudden demise,

Catboat/CINA

its present resurrection, and what is proposed for its future. *LOVE'S DANCE* is not meant to be a scholarly study of the Caymanian Catboat. We intend this work to be an introduction to one of the social foundations of this geographically isolated Island group.

A beautiful, low-sheered vessel with an almost flamboyant sail form, the Caymanian Catboat is an engineering marvel in both its hydrodynamic and its aerodynamic evolution. These small boats ventured off shore hundreds of miles to hunt and fish turtle, as well as being utilised as the Islands' waterborne pickup trucks, coasting within shallow yards of ironshore, reef and shoal beach. The Caymanian Catboat has incorporated versatility as the key to its longevity. That versatility has elevated the design from a boxy ship's boat to a sleek, no-nonsense ocean skimmer. The overall length of the boat has ranged from 14 feet to 28 feet, and presently is giving ammunition to the biggest argument between proponents for a Caymanian Catboat Class, which calls for a decision on the average length of the contemporary vessel.

Our project-to present the Caymanian Catboat to a general public-has been a task that is self-encouraging. One asks a question, and the response is so excited and fresh and stimulating that it leads to another response, equally charged, and a reference given, and a suggestion of some-body else that one just has to go see – We have had to form fairly strict parameters in our quest to present an overall Catboat documentary, for it would be easy enough to do a book of Caymanian Catboat interviews that would never end; that would propel the researcher happily scribing and taping and photographing a cultural phenomenon such as this vessel's influence upon the people of the Cayman Islands.

You will see the Caymanian Catboat and read of her, and if you are lucky, you will get to sail one. *LOVE'S DANCE – The Catboat Of The Caymans*, with its large format, splendidly nostalgic photography and interesting stories, we hope, will set you down in a Cayman Islands' seafaring tradition that will open new insights of and for an evolving Caymanian.

Today's Caymanian wishes to preserve the Caymanian Catboat, wishes to continue this hereditary vessel along its course of development and change, and wants to do it not just because of some abstract and traditional concept, but because of an almost spiritual need for a practical and challenging aesthetic. As a Caymanian competition sailor remarks, *"I cannot sail this boat as good as I can a modern boat, but I want it around long enough for me and my children to learn."*

Three Catboats/CINA

Part One: From Where and Why
CHAPTER ONE
Geography, Geology–

"There are great indications of this being the terrestrial paradise, for its site coincides with the opinion of the holy and wise theologians–all of whom agree that the earthly paradise is in the East."

– Christopher Columbus, Third Voyage of Discovery

The Caribbean Basin lies roughly between the Tropic of Cancer and the equator, about 25° to 08° of latitude, and 88° to 60° of longitude, averaging about 2000 miles from the Spanish Main to the Atlantic, and 1000 miles from Cuba to South America. The Caribbean Sea is the depository ending of the African equatorial current, while being the birthplace of the fast-flowing Gulf Stream. Nine mainland countries border this oftimes turbulent sea, while hundreds of islands under the jurisdiction of thirty or so governing islands have maintained themselves above sea level.

From a bird's-eye view, off to the left and beneath the giant wing of Cuba, are three quite isolated peaks of a great undersea mountain range-called when rising high in Cuba, the Sierra Maestra. Located approximately 200 miles from anywhere, these low-lying, orphaned peaks of granite base and dolomite covering have been given the reptilian names of turtle, lizard and finally crocodile, which in Taino, and eventually Spanish, is Caiman. The present-day Cayman Islands consist of two distinct island forms. Grand Cayman and Little Cayman are low mangrove swamp ironshore formations, with great bodies of water inside protecting coral reefs and sand shoals. Cayman Brac is a slanted bluff uprising with steep sided shores and close protecting coral reefs.

To be more specific, the Cayman Islands are the pinnacles of three underwater mountains located on the Cayman Ridge, which stretches from the Sierra Maestra of Cuba into the Gulf of Honduras. The Cayman Ridge forms the southern tectonic edge of the North American Plate. The North

Map of the Central Western Caribbean

American Plate is separated from the South American Plate by the Caribbean Plate, which is formed by the Cayman Trough, or Trench. The Cayman Trench is about 60 to 100 miles wide, and reaches a depth estimated at more than 20,000 feet.

The Cayman Ridge is an uplifted fault block, possibly the continuing result of the meeting of two side-moving transform faults, the Swan Island and the Oriente, at what is termed an 'active seismic spreading centre', the Mid-Cayman Rise. The Ridge rises 5000 to 6000 feet above the surrounding sea floor at an angle of 30° or more.

It is theorised that Grand Cayman, Cayman Brac and Little Cayman, though a part of the same Cayman Ridge, may be located on separate fault blocks, and that each has grown independent of the other. Each Island appears to have a foundation of granodiorite, succeeded by basalt and then carbonates. This last group, carbonates, is generally dolostone and limestone.

Goldfield Off George Town/CINA

3

Catboat Leaving Mother Ship/CINA

...and the Sea Turtle

"He loved green turtles and hawk-bills with their elegance and speed and their great value"

– Ernest Hemingway, *The Old Man and the Sea*

The sea turtle has the honour of being the historic reason for the habitation of the Cayman Islands. First, hunting the marine turtle, then setting up turtle-based revictualing stations brought attention, then human populations to the three-island group.

The four sea turtle species found in the Cayman Islands' geographic area are the Green Sea Turtle (Chelonia mydas), the Hawksbill Turtle (Eretmochelys imbricata), the Loggerhead Turtle (Caretta caretta) and the Leatherback Turtle (Dermochelys coriacae). Of the four, the Green Sea Turtle and the Hawksbill Turtle are the two most marketable and numerous, and the reason for the development of the Caymanian Catboat.

The Green Sea Turtle, averaging a mature weight of 300 pounds, is the largest hard-shell marine turtle. The meat of the Green Sea Turtle is an excellent source of digestible protein, while the green fat (the reason for its name) yields a fine high-grade oil. The softened shell of the Green Sea Turtle is the base for turtle soup. The tough skin around the neck of the reptile is an excellent material for the manufacture of belts.

A generally migratory reptile, the Green Sea Turtle seems to move from feeding to nesting grounds, sometimes ranging as far as a few hundred miles. The method used for migration is unknown, but magnetic fields to temperature and currents' effects have been suggested. In 1774, Edward Long commented about sea turtle migration: "-without the aid of chart or compass [they] perform this tedious navigation with an accuracy superior to the best efforts of human skill-"There are also cases of Green Sea Turtles residing in the same general location for their lifetimes.

The Green Sea Turtle is an enigma for naturalists, with contradictions and lapses of knowledge more frequent in their research than not. Except for nesting and the hatching to sea periods, the Green Sea Turtle spends its entire life in the ocean. There is no knowledge of what happens to the

In A Crawl/CINA

turtle from the time as a hatchling they enter the sea, until they reappear as immature adults in a feeding ground one to four years later. This period is called 'the lost year' and it is thought that they join Sargasso current drifts as a protective measure. The feeding group it eventually joins in this reappearance is the group it generally stays with. Another general though similar hypothesis is that when the mature female chooses a nesting ground, she will always return to that same nesting ground.

And it is the reproductive potential of the sea turtle that is responsible for its existence from well before the coming of homosapiens. Though the female sea turtle might not lay eggs for three years, when she does lay, the number of eggs can reach eight hundred.

Divine coincidence has arranged it that the mating and egg-laying seasons take place in the same seasons, twice a year, and generally at the same location. At the onset of the mating/nesting season, both sexes congregate in the same waters, usually near gradual beach areas for the Green Sea Turtle; rocky, sandy areas for the Hawksbill, and for five days enjoy association.

Thirty days after mating, the female sets her nest, first digging a pit for herself to comfortably lay upon (it might take hours to give birth). Then she will dig a pit adjoining hers for the hundred or so eggs to nestle in a protected manner. The female generally lays four clutches at fifteen-day intervals. The eggs take two or three months to hatch.

The Green Sea Turtle and the Hawksbill have quite different eating habits. The Green has a diet mainly of sea grasses and algae, with jellyfish and other invertebrates as supplemental foodstuff. The Hawksbill feeds amongst reefs and rocks, hunting sponge, mollusks, crustaceans and fish, and using the sea grasses as a supplemental. Both are extremely adaptable in diet.

One theory for the Caymans historically being a large sea turtle nesting ground but not a great feeding ground is founded upon the effects of the deep waters of the Cayman Trench producing major currents. The currents aid in the hatchling dispersal while limiting the area for shoaling sea grasses needed for feeding by both groups of sea turtle. The archipelago between Cuba and the Caymans sits on an alluvial underwater plane that gives a perfect environment for the sea grasses and the sea turtle to flourish. The shoal banks South of the Cayman Trench, stretching from Jamaica to Central America, also provide a vast area for migration, feeding and mating, and is the area most favoured by the two turtle, with the Hawksbill near Jamaica and the Green in the central area and toward Nicaragua.

Map of the Turtle Areas

Part One-From Where and Why

CHAPTER TWO

The Origin of the Caymanian Catboat
by H.E. Ross

"Among West Indian cultures, the inhabitants of the Cayman Islands are a uniquely seafaring race. While the majority of Caribbean fishermen rarely venture out of sight of land, Caymanians have always been distinctly renowned for long ranged nautical pursuits."

– Roger C. Smith,
The Maritime Heritage of the Cayman Islands, 1981

The Shallop Became the Sloop

The Turtle Islands were first logged by Ferdinand Colon and named by his father Cristobol in 1503. "We were in sight of two very small and low islands, full of tortoises, as was all the sea about-"And turtle became the reason for notice in this part of the Caribbean, as the slow-moving ships of the sixteenth and seventeenth centuries exploited other places of gold, spices and wood.

The Cayman Islands are located in a lonely stretch of sea nearly two hundred miles from Cuba to the north and Jamaica to the east, and three to four hundred miles from the western Spanish Mainland. The Taino touched upon the Islands, and later the Spanish, French, Dutch and finally the English noted the importance of these watering and victualing stations, but for some lost reason the English were the only ones to actually claim the three Islands. There was a French turtling settlement for a couple of generations in the Lesser Caymans (Cayman Brac and Little Cayman), but only the English were able to maintain a permanent settlement, first on Cayman Brac, then on Grand Cayman. The Walters, who later became the Watlers, and the Bowdens, who became the Boddens, are generally considered the first permanent families who remain to this day on the Caymans.

The British Crown Colony of the Cayman Islands has traditionally been under the administrative wing of Jamaica, until that country's independence from Great Britain in 1962. And from Jamaica came what evolved into the Caymanian Catboat.

It has been a common misconception to designate the Caymanian Catboat as a descendant of the New England Whaleboat because of the similarity in design and the sequence of emergent histories. Under mildly open scrutiny, it would seem that both vessels are descendant from the European, and/or seventeenth century Jamaican Shallop. A 1650 description of the European Shallop, or Chaloupe, is a single-masted, double-ended, undecked boat, approximately 26 feet long, eight feet wide and three feet deep.

The Jamaican Shallop's evolution saw it literally outgrowing itself before the end of the seventeenth century with a common construction size reaching 40 feet overall, and in its place the smaller Shallops became known as Sloops. Both Shallops and Sloops were employed in the hunting of turtle in the Caymans from its governing Island of Jamaica.

Henry Morgan showed a shifting in the service of Sloops by utilising them as primary attack vessels in his successful raid on Panama City in 1670. After this prosperous foray of Morgan's, the Sloop became a popular raiding vessel in the world of the privateer and the pirate.

In some circles, the Jamaican Sloop is thought to have become the transom-sterned Bermuda Sloop when Jamaican shipwrights were moved to Bermuda due to a lack of proper ship construction materials in Jamaica. The Bermuda Sloop is further thought to be the forerunner of the Baltimore Clipper.

In 1688, Sir Hans Sloane, naturalist and physician to the Governor of Jamaica, wrote, "In season some forty sloops, each with a crew of four, left Port Royal [Jamaica] for the Lesser Caymans and the Cuba Kays and returned to harbour with their catches still alive for keeping in pens and crawls."

Settlement in the Caymans by Sloane's time already had progressed to the point of official Jamaican pardons for "-deserters, debtors and privateers-"as well as having Jamaican financed forts for protection against the Spanish and French. In the Caymans, the settlers made laws for themselves, and because of this proud independence, freebooters of all nationalities made the place a neutral zone of buccaneer lawlessness.

With the merchandising of local turtle depleting their resources, Caymanian turtlers started ranging into Cuban waters with their nimble little Sloops. In 1684, two Cayman Turtle Sloops were captured by the Spanish in the Cuban Archipelago. Later that year, another six were captured in Cuban waters by the wily French, who used Cayman Sloops to capture Cayman Sloops.

The eighteenth century witnessed a reaction to Cuban protectiveness, evidenced by the shift in Caymanian turtling practices to further afield shoals and reefs off the Central American coastline. This shift called for larger craft, like schooners, to transport the nimble turtle boats. The Sloop, like the Shallop, outgrew itself as a turtling boat, to be replaced by a smaller vessel that could be carried aboard the schooner, yet had the sea-keeping abilities needed to hunt and capture turtle. The Sloop became the Caymanian Catboat.

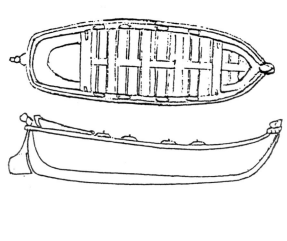

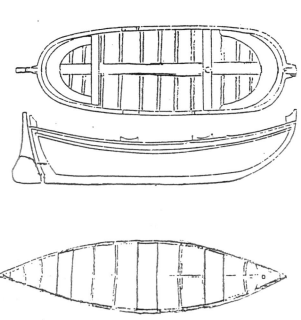

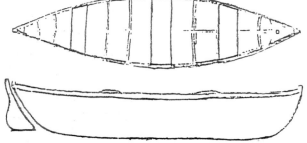

Catboat/CINA

The Contemporary Catboat
of the Caymans

"...similar to the New England whale boat but with closely spaced ribs, strong construction, excellent materials, superior workmanship."

– Edwin Doran, Jr.,
A Physical and Cultural Geography
of the Cayman Islands

A simple definition of a catboat as given in Webster's dictionary is "a boat having one mast set well forward with a single large sail."Generally what most western sailors know and recognise as a catboat is a bow-placed and fixed-stepped single-masted, wide-beamed vessel with a cut off transom, oversized rudder and a near plumbed bow. The Caymanian Catboat differs drastically from its northeastern New World cousin by being both a bow-placed and first-thwart-placed single steppable masted, narrow-beamed, double-ended, small-ruddered vessel with a spoon bow.

The typical contemporary Caymanian Catboat is at first sight a canoe-like vessel with its inherent sharp ends. Upon closer inspection, it will be noted that there is more deadrise, or upward slope angle, to the stern than to the bow, an unusual occurrence in double-enders. The Caymanian Catboat is carvel planked, each plank (seven to ten) being edge set-called set worked in the Caymans-to the other, forming a smooth siding. In size the Caymanian Catboat varies from 14 to 28 feet overall, with a beam of between three and five feet, and a draft ranging from one to two feet.

It is designed for pulling, poling, paddling, rowing and sailing, with intended duties in the areas of cargo carrying, fishing, turtling, passenger transport and recreational sailing. Though the size of the Caymanian Catboat hull varies greatly, the general concept of a practical, aesthetic form does not. A larger design is simply an enlargement of the smaller design. The sailing rigs are where the differences are most noted between the boats. Originally, it seems, the Catboat had a lug rig, or a'leg of mutton' rig. Later, the gaff and then the triangular Marconi sail form were applied. Each owner of a Catboat adapted the sail form for efficiency in the use of the particular vessel.

The woods used in construction of the vessels were Honduran white pine or Cayman cedar for planking, and the hardwoods-Cayman mahogany, plopnut, cedar, pompero, jasmine and white wood for keel, stem, sternpost and framing. The mast and boom were usually Douglas fir. The oars, or sculls, were of Cayman mahogany or mangrove, with paddles of Cayman cedar. The rudder and steering yoke were constructed in the same material as the

Crossing Muddy Foots, Little Cayman/ CINA

hull. Caymanian Catboats were fastened with trunnel dowels and screws.

A nineteen-foot Catboat weighed less than four hundred pounds, as lightweight and closely placed scantlings afforded manoeuvrability, speed and strength, while allowing the vessel to be hauled up a shore, or tackled up a schooner with relative ease. A nineteen-foot Catboat would have a nineteen- to twenty-foot mast as a minimum size, not very efficient upwind performance. and the boom would hang over the stern by about a foot as a rule of thumb. The Grand Caymanian Catboat differed from the Lesser Caymanian Catboat in that it might have a shroud to either side of the mast to support a club-footed jib for better windward ability. It might also utilise a weatherboard for balancing in a strong breeze.

With light displacement and little freeboard or draft, the Caymanian Catboat is a swift creature off the wind, but because of the same factors it is a very tender vessel, easily turned over when attempting its not very efficient upwind performance.

Grand Cayman Catboat/CINA

Chisholm Catboat/Valerie Cottier Photo

PHILATELIC COMMEMORATION

Since 1935 there have been seven issues of Cayman Islands Stamps that have featured the Caymanian Catboat. We have been fortunate in locating two.

King George V

A Caymanian Catboat was featured in the 1/2d, 2d and 1 Shilling values with a common design but different colours:

> 1/2d-ultramarine and yellow-green
> (Issued 1 May 1935)
> *(featured here)*

> 2d-ultramarine and purple
> (Issued 1 May 1935)

> 1s/-ultramarine and orange
> (Issued 1 January 1936)

King George VI *(featured here)*

A Caymanian Catboat was featured on the 1/4d (Farthing) value, which was issued on 2 October 1950

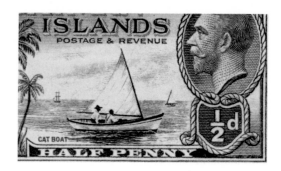

Queen Elizabeth II

Following the death of King George VI, new stamps were issued of the identical design of those issued in 1950. A portrait of Queen Elizabeth replaced the portrait of King George VI. This °d (Farthing) stamp was issued on 21 February 1955.

A new series of definitive stamps was issued on 25 November 1962, and a 1d (penny) stamp featured a Caymanian Catboat.

On 6 May 1980, a set of six stamps was issued commemorating the 1980 London International Stamp Exhibition. The 10-cent stamp featured a Caymanian Catboat, and was entitled, "Delivering Mail by Cat Boat".

The stamps featured here, with the accompanying notes, are from the collection of Mr. Ivan Burges.

Part Two: How It Is Made

CHAPTER THREE

How to Build a Traditional Caymanian Catboat

by Ira Walton

My name is Vernon Ira Walton. I was born on the 22nd day of October 1925. My mother was Malvina Bryan and my father was Captain Edwin Walton. Later, my mother married one of Captain Bryan's sons.

We are true-on Caymanian. I am third generation. All my folk originated from here except my grandmother on my father's side-she was Irish. My grandmother on my mother's side was of African descent. And my grandfather on my mother's side was Indian, about six-foot-three tall, from the Mosquito coast.

My father and my grandfather and my grandmother all came from East End. I don't know where my Irish grandmother, Jessie, came from exactly, and I don't know how she got here, but I'm happy that she did. I couldn't do this if I had wound up as somebody else.

My father, Captain Edwin Walton, was a very smart man. And I think that this can be best proven by a history book entitled, Land Of My Birth. In it you see he was a very down-to-earth person, not a big man, but he was strong, both in will and otherwise. He was the first Caymanian to get a license as Master Mariner under sail. He was also a shipbuilder, Justice of the Peace, and a legislator.

We all grew up in Cayman Brac. My father went to live there at an early age. I came to Grand Cayman to join the Army. I have been a policeman and a legislator. I've done about thirty years as a private detective, and I was a U.S. Customs officer.

We used to sail Catboats when we were little. As a matter of fact, my cousin had one called the Iz, which was about eight feet long. We used to go fishing in that, and we were only seven or eight at the time. When I was eleven or twelve, I started to go to sea. That was on schooners.

The first Catboat that I participated in building was for my brother, Albert. I was a helper for my father, who was building her. I toted water and held planks. He charged Albert twelve shillings, and he gave me two shillings out of it. Albert had to supply all the materials, so all he paid for was the labour, and in those days labour wasn't very expensive.

The Foster Catboat/Valerie Cottier Photo

Built By Ira Walton/Valerie Cottier Photo

20

Most of the Catboats in the Brac were around sixteen foot. That was the working size for Hawksbill turtling. There were a couple of famous ones that I remember: one that Lee and Uncle Dan [Jervis] did for Captain Blake Dixon, called the *Scuffler*; then there was the one that David and Lee Jervis built for themselves, called the *T.B.*, Two Brothers. They were really fast. We never would use glues. We couldn't afford it, and you wouldn't need it on those boats back then. You made it fit. My Uncle Dan, Lee and David, when they made the *Scuffler*, they made that son of a gun. When they finished, they pushed her off without a drop of paint on her, and still she never leaked a drop of water. I can't do it. They had that kind of patience. They were as slow as the grave but what they did was healthy. Not a drop of water.

Now here is a list of the woods that we used and where they were used:

Keel/Keelson-these are usually a 4 x 4"atop a 4 x 4"; pom-pero (Hypelate trifoliata), Cayman mahogany (Swietenia mahogoni), Honduran pine
Timbers (Frames, Ribs)-13/4 x 11/2"; jesme, fiddlewood (Petitia domingensis), pompero, Cayman mahogany, Cayman cedar (Cedrela odorata), plopnut (Thespesia populnea), sea grape (Coccoloba uvifera)
Planking-3/4 x 4"; spruce, cypress, Honduran mahogany, Cayman cedar, Honduran pine

Mast/Boom/Gaff-Spanish elm (Cordia gerascanthus), Douglas fir
Stem/Sternpost/Gripe/Apron-use the same woods as for the timbers
Ripling/Gunwale-Douglas fir
Thwarts-use the same woods as for the planking
Sculls (Oars)/*Paddle*-use the same woods as for the planking; pepper cinnamon (Canella winterana)
Rudder/Steering Yoke - Honduran mahogany, Cayman mahogany

The tools that were normally utilised were the #6 rip saw; the two-man saw; #10 crosscut saw; a 4-inch block plane; #4 Jack plane; a round bottom planer; spokeshave; 30-inch joiner; gouge chisels; 3/16"chisels and up.

Most of the woods are not easily accessible these days. I used to get most of my plopnut, for timbers, out of Red Bay Pond. It is an easy wood to work, not too heavy, and it's very durable. I had permission from the girl that owned that property at the time. But it was sold to a foreigner and that makes it difficult. When an outside foreigner buys land, they don't want you tramping through and cutting the trees down. It is even difficult now to get wood out of Honduras. Now we don't have anything coming here, trans-port-wise, but a plane.

Ironshore/CINA

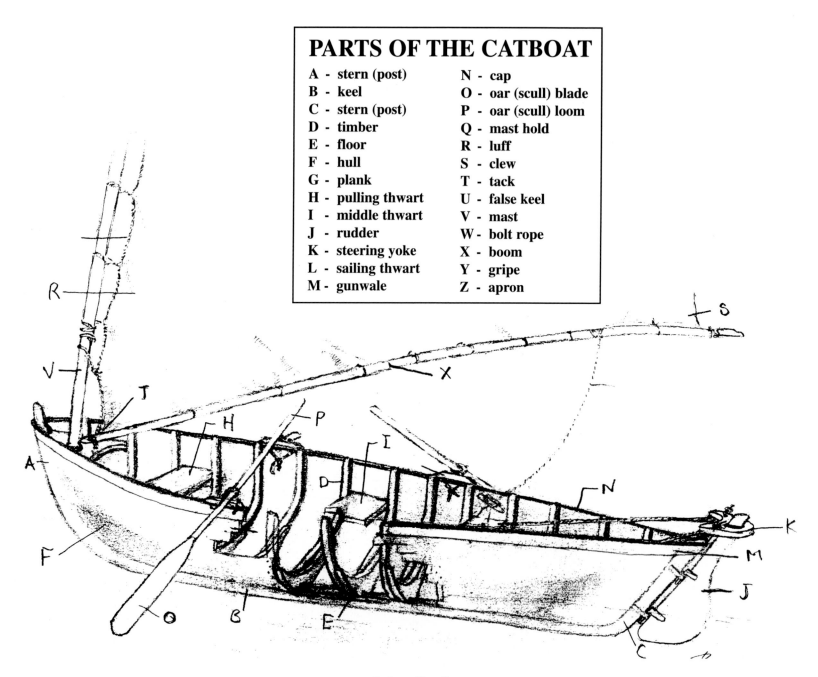

PARTS OF THE CATBOAT

A - stern (post)
B - keel
C - stern (post)
D - timber
E - floor
F - hull
G - plank
H - pulling thwart
I - middle thwart
J - rudder
K - steering yoke
L - sailing thwart
M - gunwale

N - cap
O - oar (scull) blade
P - oar (scull) loom
Q - mast hold
R - luff
S - clew
T - tack
U - false keel
V - mast
W - bolt rope
X - boom
Y - gripe
Z - apron

Catboat Detail

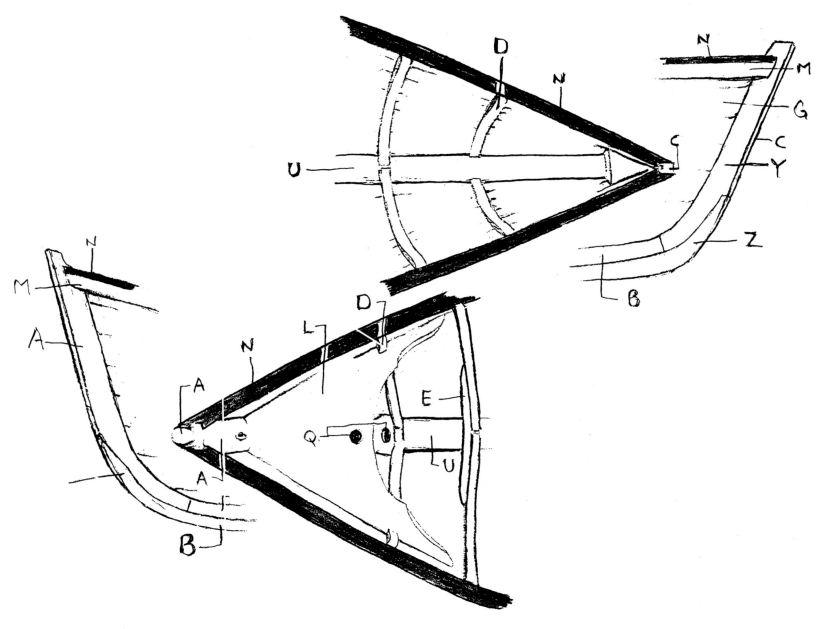

Catboat Bow and Stern Detail

There is plenty of sea grape, but when you use it you have got to be careful because it warps quickly. You cut it down, flatten it, and the day you need to use it you soak it in salt water. You can't let it hang around in the sun because it will go off on you. You have to put it in quick.

To Build a Catboat

You have to make a half model, which you carve by hand and eye; then cut down the centreline in half. You cut it into sections, for argument's sake, let's say, on a scale of one-half inch to a foot (1/2"=1'). You cut the sections where the timbers go, say sixteen sections. You take those sections and you lay them on a piece of paper and you trace it onto the paper. Then you mark the waterline at one-half inch from the bottom. I start at the top and measure the width, say one inch, which equals two feet (on the half); then you measure down at 1/2-inch increments. The spacing between timbers is usually thirteen to fourteen inches. Then you measure this all out in feet on a sheet of paper. Then you transfer the measurement onto and cut templates of thin plywood. You set the plywood up and batten them around. It's called a spoiling batten, about a half-inch wide. You mark it at each level, which leaves you with the full size shape.

Now you have set up the boat for the keelson, to have the exact length of the keelson. I lay the 4 x 4" keelson down and put a 3/8"or 1/2"bevel along the piece. On that same level you slot out a piece to set the stem or stern post. You bolt or trunnel them in place.

For the stem you can rabbet the edge to set the plank ends in, or you can bring it right alongside and put a gripe on it. The gripe is a piece of wood that covers the edge of the planks, running parallel to the stem post. You have to put stopwaters of soft pine on the two sides at the bottom so moisture can be released. The apron passes over the joining to cover it. The apron goes down to tie the stem and the keelson together also. Then you shape it all.

I used to take the templates into the Pond and find the tree that crooked closest to its shape to cut for the timbers. You need that natural bend. It might be a little off, wider, but when you cut the bark off and flatten it, well, it takes a little experience and practice to see the shape. Those timbers are then put into place, about thirteen to fourteen inches apart. The closer you put those timbers the less chance the boat has of opening.

The *Ajax* was another famous Cayman Brac Catboat. The *Ajax* was nineteen feet, eleven inches long, a big son of a gun for a Cayman Brac Catboat. My father made her. Dan Jervis designed her, he and his oldest son Lee. Then my father and his oldest son, Harris, made her. They made the *Ajax*. She was designed for both sailing and cargo. Now I have built three off the model of that *Ajax*. I have her frames in my workshop. I think my father made her in 1934, 1935.

It was after 1932 anyway. She was good for about fifty, fifty-five years. The spacing of the timbers on the *Ajax* is fourteen inches centre to centre.

If you are using one-inch planking on the same size boat, your timbers would be bigger, and you could put them farther apart because the spaces in between are strengthened by the thickness of that planking. The thinner the planking, the closer the timbers.

The width of the planking starts at four inches in the bow to three inches in the middle to generally two inches in the stern. The bottoms are almost all the same, so when they are racing, it's man against man, not boat against boat.

The 'ripling' is the decorative-appearing plank, 3/4" thick by 31/2" wide, that covers the upper edge of the sheer plank and butts against the head of the timbers. The gunwale, or cap, covers the ripling and the sheer plank edge but not the timber tops. The gunwale is 3/4"thick and 11/2" wide. If the gunwale gets a little tough in bending when fitting it, I put it in a little hot water and bend it on around. I screw it to the sheer plank and ripling. Then you round the timber top edges and it all fits nicely. The ripling is then painted white and the gunwale is painted black. You actually widen the black down onto the ripling a half-inch-makes the boat look lower.

The one-inch planking is really just three-quarter inch, but for the turn of the bilge they used to use five-quarter inch wood to have the extra for gouging out the rounding. Now we use two pieces and it leaves a little seam up top. But it is not something you can rush.

My father told me, "You want something neat, you do it slow. You want something rough, you do it fast."

The stem and the stern posts are three and a half inches on the inside and two to an inch and a half on the outside. You start out with a 4 x 4" piece of wood and work it down.

The keel is attached to and under the keelson and joined by the aprons. It is tapered from four inches at the keelson to two inches at the bottom.

You make a pattern for the rudder on paper, the same for the steering yoke. The yoke should be at least eighteen to twenty-four inches, because the wider it is, the less strain it takes to pull that rudder.

The sculls, or oars, do not have a standard size, but are about six or seven feet long, including the blade on the loom. The best were made from pepper cinnamon wood because it stood up to the sea. The loom is tapered and then flattened to receive the blade, and a groove is notched in the blade to fit the loom. And then you simply tie them together, screw or nail them. I put brass screws from the back of the loom on into the blade. If I could not afford brass screws, I'd drive nails through and clench them back. That would be a rough job, though.

We call oars sculls, because oars use oarlocks and our sculls use a strap. You have a ballot, which is a piece of hardwood secured atop the gunwale and timberheads. You loop a strap through that, and the loom of the scull is inserted through the strap for rowing.

The paddle is mostly made of mahogany, Honduran or Cayman. It has a horn carved into the top to hold it good; then you taper it down to a good holding place about two, two and a half feet down. The paddle is about four or five feet. The blade tapers from twelve inches to about six inches. It is all one piece.

The mast should be the length of the boat. The boom should set twelve inches over her sternpost. To set your mast right, you should be able to put a plumb bob on it that would sit right in the middle of your pulling thwart for holding into the wind. The pulling thwart is the front rowing thwart. There are usually four thwarts, two middle thwarts, a stern sheet thwart and the pulling thwart.

Catboats are not easy to sail. You have to know how to balance that son of a gun. And you have to have the feel. It isn't something that you get by looking in a book. You've got to be there on that gunwale a long time- You have got to get the feel of her. If you hold her rudder over too hard when going into a sea, you can flip her over real fast. You have to let off and ease her over. You have to sail her real easy, easy, easy.

Sometimes we would put an additional false keel on the Catboats. We would not actually fasten it on securely. We put it on so it could come off easily, a bolt or screw forward and aft. That was to keep her up, sail closer to the wind, and not drift away. And we, from Cayman Brac, did not use a weatherboard; we would get out on the gunwale. The captain would be there steering with a long yoke line. They are quick boats, boy.

Bowse's Bluff/CINA

Catboat/CINA

The Best Race Is the One You Win

by Gleason Ebanks

My name is Gleason Ebanks. I was born right here in West Bay, Boatswain's Bay to be exact. I was born on the 28th of August 1928. Last August I was seventy years old. My grandparents on my father's side-his father was named Aemon Ebanks and my grandmother was named Amelia Ebanks. My grandparents on my mother's side were Joe and Susan Ebanks. My father was Elvin and my mother was Florrie. They called her Florrie for Florence.

I was around boats from when I was very small, and those days there was only sailing boats to get hold of. There weren't any powerboats. Everywhere we went we were either under sail or paddles or oars. If the wind wasn't too kind, you oared it; if the boat was too big, you .... drifted.

I first started sailing when I was ten years old. And the first time I went fishing alone in a Catboat was with my father along the beach. I grew up in the Barkers area. He stayed on the beach and watched me out in the boat. I was alone out there fooling around with her. If I had gotten into trouble he would have been there to come help me. But I used to make it pretty good.

I had started to go fishing in small boats with friends, older people, like my Uncle Steven, who were fishermen. After those experiences I just kept working at boats.

Around here we used to have our own little races, our own little regattas on the weekends out on North Sound. On Friday or Saturday evening there would be five or six of us out there. We'd work them to improve them, to see who could get the fastest. I used to do a lot of sailing on small boats. Then I went on schooners and went down to Nicaragua.

The first time I went down to Nicaragua on a turtle schooner was when I was fourteen years old. The Jemson carried us over. We were ranging, staying on the cays, actually a place called Mawson Dennis. It's got a different name on the chart, but everybody called it Mawson Dennis. There was no dry land there, just big clumps of big red mangrove bush. We had to build huts over the water. We stayed there a few weeks and caught a few turtle and came home.

I went a couple of more trips ranging. I went to Dead Man Bar with Will Powery, as cook. A ranger works independent of the schooner on a Catboat.

Off Galleon Beach/Eziethamae Bodden

I was ranging one time in 1952 and we got caught in a heavy nor'wester. It blew 95 miles an hour-a hurricane, actually. It was bad weather. I went about thirty-odd miles out in that open Catboat. I didn't get where I wanted to go, so I had to go somewhere else. That was in a big Catboat, twenty-four feet long.

We went to the nets that morning and picked up ten turtle, and I started to head back into the huts from where we were ranging. I was riding her in by jib because the main boom had busted. The sails had gotten so out of proportion that I could not hold the wind that I wanted, but the others wanted to leave the main up. It was kind of smooth there in the lee of shore, so we tried to pull the boat against the current but we couldn't get ahead-we were going astern. We started to make for somewhere else, but couldn't make that either. The boat filled up on us once, then twice, but didn't go down. She just got a lot of water in her. We got her bailed out and dumped three turtle to lighten her up.

We finally went to Mosquito Cay where the bigger schooners were, but it was a very bad day. The Adams, which was a big schooner, and was under power; she had an engine. Well, she could normally cruise at ten miles an hour. That day she could barely do three miles an hour. They tell me that that day she had water on deck up to your knees coming off the fishing ground.

Another one that was a big, big boat was named *Anteres,* and when she would drop into a sea and squat her stern, the water would come over her stern and go down into the cabin. The engineer had to stay down in the engine room because when she would raise up with the sea, her propeller would clear the water and she would rev up, so he had to stay down there to slow the engine down so as not to break a shaft or something. It was a bad day.

We would get some smooths that day crossing to Mosquito Cay, but for the last twelve miles we were in the big open water, in some big seas. I've been in some hurricanes in freighters and big ships, but nothing was like that terrible day in an open boat. I had the jib up and about four foot of mainsail up the mast. I was going more with the wind then, going downwind almost, and she was going with the sea, just going.

There were six of us on the Catboat that day because when we left that morning we were expecting to get some heavier weather. We had a smaller boat with us but we left her at the huts, and the six of us went in the bigger boat. We didn't have a name for that Catboat. She belonged to the Merrens, and we used to call her the *High Head.*

Ours was a Grand Caymanian Catboat, and the difference between a Caymanian Catboat and a Brac Catboat was, though they would have been built the same, here on Grand

Regatta/CINA

Cayman, we would put them as sloop rigs. They looked different because of that. Everything else was the same. The Cayman Brackers always had the sail up in the bow. When you rig them like ours, it is really a sloop rig, but it was still built as a Catboat. Sometimes they called the Brac boats 'Crank-style,' because when the sail is set in the head, it is easier to crank, or tip, over.

The Brackers also used to put their sail high in the foot, high off the rail. We used to cut our sails to go low to the rail, but they used to cut theirs high because they used to look for turtle when they fished, and they cut their sails high so they could see overboard.

We have our mainmast in the sailing thwart because we fancy that the Catboat sails better with it there. It is easier to handle. With the mast in the bow you couldn't protect the mast, but using the thwart you could protect the mast with rigging. In the head, there isn't anywhere to put spreaders. Our way you could use a lighter and taller mast and protect it with spreaders and rigging down along the sides like a yacht. Sometimes I would have three layers of rigging.

Sometimes, if the mast was too short and you wanted to use a taller mainsail, you could put a yardstick up at the top. You could cut it so there was enough below the top, more below than above, so as not to overbalance it. Then you would attach your halyard to the yardstick. When you raised the sail, the stick would bring the sail up, and when you lowered it, the yardstick would bring the sail down. Usually the masts were the same length as the boat.

You would protect the jib with a boltrope sewn around the whole sail usually. I used to have a small wire sewn in the front of my jib to keep it tight, so it wouldn't lean out. With the jib stick you must have more than two-thirds of the stick inside the hull. When you adjust the sheet, the luff forms better for better control. The sail is attached at the bow by lashings.

A weatherboard was placed just a few feet aft of the sailing thwart. Sometimes, so the guys could put their hands on the rigging to steady themselves, it would be placed just aft the mast. But normally, it was just forward of the middle thwart. When sailing alone you could handle the sheets and steer from the weatherboard. But most of the time the man steering the boat, the captain, handles the jib. He doesn't have to trouble the main much. The guys sailing, the crew, would handle the board.

I always made my steering yoke lines so they would come to the middle of the boat so if you wanted to move further forward you can control the course.

To rig the boat in the water you first step the mast. The sailing thwart has a hole in it and there is another hole directly beneath on the keelson. You stick the mast end into

Regatta/CINA

both holes. If the mast was real heavy you would place the mast bottom right at the hole and start straightening it up by walking forward. When it is in, you attach the rigging.

If it is a small sail, you have it attached to the mast, but if it is a big sail you leave it down until the mast is rigged. Then the sail is attached to the hops that are always on the mast, and to the halyard and raised. The boom is laced to the sail and has a crutch that fits the mast. You rig the sheets. When you hoist the sail up you slack the sail until you are ready to go sailing, then you trim the sail and go about your business.

The Cayman Brac Catboats are smaller and use smaller stuff, so their sail is all attached. They just stick the mast in at a hole at the head and let the boom and sail down. To take it down they just put the sail up to the mast and take the mast out and lay it down.

The average length for the old-time Catboats was from 16 to 18 feet. The later years, the guys were building them twenty to twenty-four feet. Twenty to twenty-four feet became common in the last years of Cayman Catboat building. And I consider the last years to be in the 1950s.

I was about nineteen years old when I started to race, fifty-one years ago. We started racing for the fun of it, just the fun. When Mr. Bertie started the races down in West Bay, he had a cup, a silver cup, and gave a couple of shillings to the winner. You got the cup if you won the race, but if you won the race two out of three years, the cup was yours. I hold the cup.

Mr. Bertie organised the race for Easter Monday. Later, he had it along Seven-Mile Beach. First we would sail up to the Northwest Point; then after the years went by, we would go over to the Beach Club; then from the Royal Palms, the Galleon Beach, different places. Then we got bigger boats. My first boat wasn't but sixteen feet long-called her the Wireless. But we used to have the best races in the North Sound because there was a true wind all the time. You could hardly see the shore for all the people come to see the races.

I did not win all my races, because sometimes I would sail in other people's boats, but I never lost in the Delco. I picked the Delco up in the early 1960s.

She was built in West Bay by a man named Ewans Hydes, and she was owned by Aaron Powery. They used to carry her down to Nicaragua for ranging. Another man, Captain Joe Anglin, bought her from Aaron, and I bought her from him. Then I fixed her up.

I fixed the Delco up for racing. She was a good sailer anyhow. But they never did have any good sails on her. When they used her turtling, they never did put a good sail on her, just a little small sail. What I still saw her doing with that little sail made me know that she was a good sailer.

Regatta/CINA

I changed her model a little bit; I changed her bow a little bit. And I changed her stern a little bit, not much. I flared her head a little bit so she would be a more sea kindly sea vessel, and she would be a little better looking. And I fiberglassed her and bought good sails, Dacron® sails, and stainless steel rigging. I made a mast out of some pieces of wood. I made her just for racing.

Sometimes I would put her in the water for a few days, but not normally. I kept her in the yard. If I had a race on South Sound I would take her there in the truck, and after the race I would load her back onto the truck and take her back to the yard. I had a garage made for her. If there was a race the next week in the Sound, I might leave her there, but normally I would take her home after I had down the race. She was twenty-one feet, seven inches long.

The guy who was working with me when I was changing her, he loved her. He always wanted her, so I was getting kind of busy, and racing, Catboat racing, had kind of gone. Well, he wanted her, so I gave her to him. He raced her a few times, then he got on a ship and got lost up around Africa. He had hauled Delco up and put her in his yard around Mount Pleasant where he lived. He got lost, and never came back. The boat just stayed there. After she started to drop down, they just took her and dumped her somewhere. When I asked about her, they said they had dumped her. I was going to get her and take her back, fix her. But they said they had dumped her.

Knob/Clifford Ashley

1973 Regatta, The Delco/Eziethamae Bodden

CHAPTER FOUR

A Lady Catboat Captain
by Valma Hew

My full name is Lorna Valma Walton Dilbert Hew. I was named after a boat that my father sailed on, the Lady Valma, up around New York. He was a cook aboard her. John Crosby Walton was my father's name. Who knows if it was really New York. In those days everythin 'up there' was New York or Tampa or Miami.

I was born in Spot Bay, Cayman Brac on the 23rd of January 1928. My grandparents on my father's side were Elizabeth and Lemuel Walton. On my mother's side were Clarissa and Captain Theopholis Ritch.

I was nine or ten years old when I was sailing my first Catboat. They were just regular, small Catboats with one mast and one sail. They thought, when I was young, that I was on the masculine side because I enjoyed doing the things that boys would do instead of the sewing and knitting I was supposed to enjoy doing. I learned all that-I had to-but I liked to live fast, so I did not like the sewing and knitting. I liked the sea.

Women generally thought I was crazy. My parents quarreled with me a lot about sailing. My mother said, "One of these days you will not come back." But then in the Brac, men were always at sea, so most of the women had to do our own fishing. Most women would fish from the shore, but I preferred the Catboat. There were two of us sailing back then. Havilah Jackson, I think, had her own boat, and she just lived on the water, out there all day and part of the night. I have a feeling that she even built her own boat, and if not, her brothers, Moses and Frankie, helped her. She was younger than I was.

The boys used to make fun of me and I was always bashful of boys. When all the other girls were dressing up, and with lipstick, I was in overalls. I was a tomboy, but I was extremely shy. I think that shyness comes from when we were poor, very, very poor. What I had to wear was what my aunt sent second-hand from the United States, and that's how I learned to sew, to cut them over. I was very proud of them but I know there was probably a lot of snickering behind my back, because everybody knew they were second-hand.

One thing, though, I had a lot of fun being a tomboy. The boys would make fun of me, but I did not stop it. I would swim for hours. I would fish on my Catboat. Children should be free and relaxed and do what they like best.

I liked the sailing. I like it when there is lots of wind and they have to get up on what we call the mountin', that's the weather side when the sail is pulling. Then you have to

In The Blue Light/CINA

move from that side to the other when you change course. You have to keep her stern in the water. That was the joy to me, a challenge, since Catboats are so easily turned over.

Very seldom would we use a weatherboard, only if the wind was very, very strong. In my growing up days, I had seen them doing it, but generally if it was real strong weather, three of us would go out for the weight. Wood was too scarce to get that extra piece for a weatherboard.

Uncle Edwin Walton built most of the boats then. Then his son took over, Kerry, then Ira picked it up. They all lived in Bogey Sand. There was also Haverd and Arthur Dilbert. My grandfather built bigger boats, two-masters, even three-masters, schooners, the builders being Ashton Reid and Haverd Dilbert.

I was fourteen years old on my first turtling voyage. It was January and I was allowed to go there to pick Eggbird and Noddi eggs. I went with my mother and stepfather to the Serrano Bank Cay. They had lived there for many years and would come home for Christmas. It was great.

They'd go there to turtle. The cay was about a mile and a half long, and a half mile wide. I would walk that cay ten to twelve times per night looking for turtles. They would crawl up to lay. It was fun there.

May, June, July was the Eggbird season, so my grandfather would take lots of boys over from April or May to pick eggs, which he would take over to Kingston, Jamaica, to sell. He used to sell them to a huge man named Mister Whiteside. It was my grandfather's schooner, Captain Theo Ritch, with his brother Joe Ritch-we called him Uncle Joe-they built her, the schooner, the Taylor. There was Uncle Joe, Uncle Edwin and Arthur Dilbert, who built the Taylor. I don't remember her size exactly, but to me, back then, she was just huge.

My grandfather would let me steer her. He would leave me alone there. I wasn't allowed to handle the sails and lines, though. And I would cook. I would take care of the bunks, clear the bunks and make them up.

Every three weeks we'd go back and forth, Jamaica to Serrano Cay. We'd have crates of eggs on top of each other, taller than me. Tons and tons of eggs, Eggbird eggs and Noddi eggs.

I sailed the Catboats on Serrano to go fishing, or to go over to the other small cays to see if there would be turtle eggs. They wouldn't be more than two miles away.

Now they say there are a lot of sharks there, but I don't remember any, or many back then. I lived in the water. You would see the occasional shark, but not like what I am hearing these days. But back then there was deep water between Serene and the Triangle, and that was very sharked, very much full of sharks. That is very, very deep water....

The Kirk B -A Brac Schooner/CINA

My uncle was out there in one of those heavy storms-I think it was 1932, a hurricane. He had to bury himself in a barrel and put air pipes up. That's how he survived. Nobody else survived it.

Serrano Cay has fresh water, very clean, sweet water. It never had any trees, though-shrubs and a lot of white sand. The west end is all high rocks and the south side had a bit of rock, too. The lighthouse was there on top of the higher rocky part.

We had huts to live in, built of thatch with no flooring. We slept in hammocks and some had bunks, but the hammocks were the safest because there were lots of crabs, and they could crawl up the bunks.

The only women that I remember were my mother and I out there. My mother stayed out there on the cay year after year, picking eggs and catching turtle with her husband, my stepfather. I did not get to go until I was fourteen. I had to go to school, but at fourteen you were out of school. From then on I could go for about three months, June, July, August, hurricane season. Then my grandfather would make the trip to Jamaica. We did not think about hurricanes then.

The Noddis used to lay in January, February and March, but their eggs were not as popular as the Eggbird eggs, which were very expensive. Noddi eggs were a shade bigger. We would get turtle eggs also, but we could not save those. The red ones we could try to dry and sell, but the white ones did not have anything in them, just slime, so they were thrown away. Normally, if the captured turtle was ready to lay, we would bury those and let them hatch.

I used to make a crawl, like turtle tracks. It was wicked of me, to fool my stepfather into thinking they had found a turtle nest, and they would dig it out. I would crawl on the beach in the night and make the track exactly like that of a turtle. I would carry a shovel and dig a hole and fill it back up. That was my fun. My stepfather would get very upset.

When I first started sailing Catboats I did it a little bit at a time, and it was not too very hard that way. I used to go in the boats so often with my stepfather whenever he'd go out fishing. Then one day I took one out on my own. I would go out fishing or just go sailing, if the weather was not too bad. I would not sail out too far, maybe down to Stake Bay Point. I sailed even after I got married, and tried to teach my son, Armand Dilbert, who is now a great seaman.

I stopped sailing after my first husband died. We used to go out sailing a lot together. He was killed, and it was a very sad time for me. I didn't know what to do, and I gave up everything. It was not long after that that I moved here to Grand Cayman and just started working. After that I didn't have any more to do with a Catboat. It was gone for me.

Captain Theo's Four Master/CINA

Master Mariner

by Captain Paul Hurlston

I am Paul Hurlston, born in South Sound, Grand Cayman on January 11, 1931. That give me sixty-eight years this year.

My father did not go to sea. All of my five brothers did. I was the youngest one and-well, it was the only way to make a living. My grandfather was the, or one of the best turtle pilots. His name was Captain Charles Bush. He owned three vessels, schooners. He could not read or write but he had ambition. You could hardly live with him but he was a good fisherman and he was honest. As everybody said back then, whatever you earned you got. In those days it wasn't wages, it was shares. You catch so many turtle, you sell them, all expenses are paid. What was left was shared out. He went down in history not just as a very honest man, but also as a very disagreeable one, Charles Christopher Bush.

There were two Charles Bushes and both were captains, so my grandfather was known as Black Charles Bush, and Errol Bush, the present Port Authority Director, his grandfather was called White Charles Bush. That was so not to confuse them because they were both turtle fishermen and captains started sailing with a trip to the Nicaraguan coast to catch turtle. That was January 10, 1946. I went under my old uncle, Carl Bush, who is still alive while I am writing this story, at ninety-six years old. It was rough work back then. We caught 200 turtle and my share was forty-eight pound Sterling. I was rich, man. At fifteen years of age in 1946 with forty-eight pound, I was rich.

And the following year, in January, I had saved that money to pay my way down to the United States. It was January 9th, and I left here to go to Tampa. I was only sixteen and they said nobody would hire me. We worked under British Registry and so we had to go to the British Consulate in Tampa to get signed off. They would not sign you off if you were under eighteen. But I was fortunate that day; I had already had a ship but had to go through this formality with the British Consulate. Well, he was in a meeting and the secretary, she signed me off. And I have been going to sea ever since. I went as high as I could go, Master, for thirty and a half years.

I remember one Catboat; she was built by Elroy Arch. She was a big boat, I think, twenty-eight, thirty-foot. She was beautiful and she could sail. We were ranging on the cays, fishing from the cays, Man O'War Cay. We would sail

Three Men/CINA

Filling Up/CINA

sometimes ten miles away in that big old boat carrying fifteen turtle. She did not have a name. Turtlefishing Cats used to be at least eighteen feet long.

I was just fifteen years old, very skinny, and had to man those big red mangrove oars. My uncle, he was rough. He was always in a hurry and expected me to do the same work that a seasoned man would do. But you know what? That prepared me for all of what I would meet for the rest of my days. Nothing could be harder. That toughened me up, and- I survived.

In the fishing grounds out there, the old fishermen never fished on Sundays. Saturdays they would take up their nets. Monday morning early you start again to set the nets. The places they used to put the nets they called 'sets,' and if the weather was favourable, the schooners would anchor under the lee of a cay or shoal. The next morning before daylight they would go out to take in the nets. The advantage of having a large Catboat was if you had fifteen, twenty turtles you could bring them all in at one time. Otherwise you have to make a lot of fast trips. As soon as the sun comes up, the turtle start to misbehave. He wants to get free of the net. He can be tangled in the net, but while it's dark he sleeps. But when the sun comes up he's a fighter, and he wants to be free of that net. If you had a small boat, you have to make too many trips. You lose time.

I think the Catboat we have with its double end was developed to be manoeuvrable. This type of Catboat was first built on Cayman Brac, and they did a lot of trapping, trapping the Hawksbill Turtle. You had to have something that could turn on a dime. You could go astern. By the boat being a double-ender, you could just back her to reverse direction very quickly. You could manoeuvre to trap the Hawksbill. I was told that the first guy that built the Catboat was a guy named Jervis from Cayman Brac, and I think the first one on Grand Cayman was owned by McGovern Watler of East End.

And then my first cousin, John Hurlston, he was a very young guy when he revolutionised building Catboats. He died when he was twenty-five years old, but today you could probably still find one or two boats he built, and that was back in the '30s. Before him, they all planked the boats from the sheer strake down, but he turned the hull up and started from the garboard strake and went back up to the sheer. He is the first person who did that.

The same guy built a Catboat for the Chisholms of North Side, because before roads, that was the transportation from North Side across the Sound. That was a big boat, I remember. She was a huge Catboat.

When we were growing up the Catboats were used in the races and the regattas. That was a beautiful sight, to see ten or twelve boats racing under sail. And the skill in sailing them, that should be preserved. That is an art.

Chisholm Catboat/Valerie Cottier Photo

Catboat/CINA

Catboats Beaching/CINA

The Last Generation?

by Captain Ashton DeOsca

I was born in West Bay, Grand Cayman. Grew up in the U.S. I am a professional mariner.

My grandfather was a skipper. His father was a skipper. All his life he sailed. Most of my brothers did. I came up in the family and went to sea and sailed. Paul and I have sailed together. We were all professional seamen.

My father's name was Captain DeOsca Ebanks also. They called him Captain DeDe.

This is part of the reason behind our Seafarers' Association-to preserve the maritime history of the Islands. The Cayman Islands today are the result of what a maritime heritage did for the economy, and if we don't preserve it now there will be nobody interested enough to do it later. We are probably the last generation of Cayman Island seamen. The younger generations are not involved in real seamanship or sailing. It is not necessary for them to do it. For our generation it was necessary. It was a way of life, of making a living. Not so much even in my generation because I came along when things were getting better. It is the foundation of the economy of the Cayman Islands. We were seamen and a seafaring people, whether it was turtle fishermen, local fishermen, or deep sea, they did all that was available in order to make a living and support their families. Tourism, banking and construction were not here. This came in the '70s. That is when the economy of the Island started to change and become more prosperous. There were only a couple of hotels here in the late '50s, but there were very few visitors even for those.

I went to sea at nineteen. I went to the old Cayman high school; then I went to New York to finish school. Then I came back and settled for a while and got married. I started with National Bulk Carriers in 1958 as a mess man. That went on for a while. Then I got to the deck department; then went to maritime school and received a license as an officer and continued on from there. I have a Master's License and I have sailed as a Master. My last eight years I was port captain and operations manager at the Port of Mobile, Alabama.

My first contact with Catboats was with a boat that my grandfather owned called the Waltzpint. They called her a dory, and she was probably around thirty feet. She was very well equipped for sail. They would actually go to the cays with that vessel. She would go in company with one

Goldfield/CINA

Weighing Turtle/CINA

The Catch/CINA

of the small sailing ships. They would take a limited amount of gear and go along in company with the other vessel on her rounds.

The Catboat had no name, but because of her size, she could carry more turtle to bring back to the mother ship. We called the bigger vessel the mother ship, who would collect the people and their turtle and take them to their crawls, or whatever they put them in for the three, four or five weeks or months, until they were ready to load them back on board.

That was my first Catboat.

My father had quite a few of them; he had quite a number of Catboats. They were between fifteen and nineteen feet and they used them for turtling.

We also used them for local fishing-towing, we called it. They call it trolling now.

As kids, I remember taking one of my cousins on my uncle James' side-Uncle Jimmy we called him. He had a nice little boat called the Bluenose. Well, my cousin Robert and I, we were pretty close together, about twelve, eleven or twelve years old. On this Sunday morning, we took that boat early and went towing with it, and we came back with the biggest wahoo, or queenfish, that you ever had seen.

Uncle Jimmy, he met us on the dock. Never said a word. But if we had not had that big fish, we would have been dead meat for taking that boat out without permission that Sunday, I tell you. The thing was, it was just the two of us. It took the two of us just to get the mast up. We were healthy, but those masts were heavy. They were made of pine. Most of the masts were made out of white pine or white wood or some local hardwood that they've got around here. It was formed by hand plane, rounded by hand.

The Catboat experience is where most Caymanians, at least of our age group, had their first sea knowledge, sailing Catboats, fishing Catboats, or even if just for pleasure. I think there is still a reason for its existence. Even if put into a yacht style, or whatever, it could be used as a heritage thing, and also have a daily use as a fishing boat. There are many local fishermen-though now everybody's got fiberglass boats-who could still do the same thing with a planked boat. I think it should be preserved in its original state. With traffic now, most of those Catboats could beat the commute with a good breeze.

The importance that the Catboat had on the Island was that it was the dependable means of transportation for your family's support. It was the fishing vessel, and in conjunction with the larger sailing vessels, be it turtling or cargo, it sustained the economy of the Islands.

I think the Caymanian Catboat should be preserved simply because of the heritage and usefulness of it. It still has a role, among the local population anyway, and I think that if people had the opportunity to buy one they would get one. Even if they already have pleasure boats and speedboats, they would probably still use the Caymanian Catboat.

Regatta/CINA

Sailing With a Bracker Tomboy

By Havilah Jackson

My name is Havilah Elizabeth Jackson. I am 73 years old and was born right here in this house on the 1st of July 1926. This house was built in 1921. It was turned around and moved over a hundred feet by the hurricane of 1932.

My father's name was Captain Thomas Solomon Jackson and my mother was Gertrude Lenasha Ebanks. She was from West Bay, Grand Cayman. She was not a Bracker.

My father was a captain who used to go to sea out of here on Cayman Brac, but during the War he was called to Jamaica to build wooden minesweepers. Before that, he built ships and Catboats, and he owned Catboats. He used to give out his Catboats to the men who went turtling for shares of their catch.

The Brackers fished Hawksbill Turtle because of the shell. The shell is what England wanted in those days. They used to ship them to Jamaica and then they would be shipped from Jamaica to England. With the Green Turtle you only had the meat, also the Loggerhead. But with the Hawksbill you got the meat and the shell.

You use the Catboat to chase the Hawksbill until he tires and stops. You keep an eye on him with the waterglass. Then you let the net down to get him. His fins will hook into the net. The net is conical with an iron hoop at the bottom. There are sinkers attached to the bottom hoop, and a long line attached to the top ending. I rowed backwards and was guided by my brother, Moses, as we would chase him until he got tired and would lay there to rest. Then we would trap him. The net is called a trap net. I did not trap; I rowed. My brother did the trapping.

I can't remember when I started on Catboats. Since my father built them, it must have been at a very early age. He used to carry us out to set and pull up fish pots. He didn't fish with line, just pots. He would put one down today and tomorrow he would pull it up and set another. And he always used to carry us with him.

My favourite boat was the last boat my father owned. He used to call her Time. She was a small boat. He made her small so that his girls could handle her. Maybe twelve feet. He said he built her that size so that me and my sister would always have a boat to use and it would not be too much weight to pull up.

I sailed it. Hoisted up the sail, held the yoke line and sat on the rail there. Every time the breeze would take the sail and swing it down, you just hang back on the rope and bring her back. Sometimes I'd just use the paddle to steer with.

The Blue Light/CINA

Valma and I fished together sometimes but most of the time she was alone. Other times she would go alone and I would go alone. Or at times me and my brother Moses would go, or me and my sister would go out fishing. There were other women fishing off Catboats, such as Leona Sanford down in the Bight and Lina Dixon Smith. They both still go fishing but now with skiffs. But at the time, Catboats were all we had. It is not too many years since outboard motors have come in. Before then, it was just oars and sails. Fishing is why the Catboats were sharp on both ends. It was so you could reverse them easily. Turtle fishing and fishing.

They used to call us tomboys. At the time they didn't say queers or lesbians. They would say, 'You are going to be a tomboy. You better stop and think, and look toward your feminine side.' I would just say, 'You wait, you will see.' They thought there was too much of this rough stuff; it is time for you to turn into a lady. Get yourself dressed up. I would answer, 'I will dress up when I want to go out, when there was a reason to go out.' And when I did dress up, the boys would look at me even more, because they were used to seeing me dressed all rough.

We had the babies. The men were out to sea and we the women had to feed the children. And most of the men who went to sea never came back. They were lost at sea and they left families, children. Everybody had to try to help each other. My father lost two brothers in 1932. So everything we had we had to share with their wives and children. Whenever we caught some fish, we would share them.

I would go out and pull pots myself alone. A pot is four by four by two feet, and weighs about eighty to a hundred pounds with fish and weights in it. But it's easy to come in, to haul up. You haul it up easily, but at the surface, when you want to lift it out of the water, that's when the weight takes you. You have to know what you are doing then, because the Catboat can go over. You have got to lean low, then you haul back to the other side of the boat, shift your weight to the other side. If you keep your weight over the pot's side, you and it will end up in the water. So you just keep leaning back. You catch it by one corner, and if you can get that over the gunwale, you slide it on in. That's the way they did turtle, too.

I liked the boat itself. Somehow, you just felt good. It was a good feeling to be off and look back at the land. I

Three Men In A Catboat/CINA

would just sit there, and she would drift, and I would just look back at the shore. It was a beautiful sight.

I remember a day that Moses and I went out with the boat and we had a crocus sack sail. We were trolling, and he hooked on a barracuda, a big one, but we did not have sufficient line. So he tied on some thatch string, but it wasn't strong enough and the string broke. We lost that barra, which was about three feet or so.

Another time, with my oldest brother, because he wasn't a boat man, well, instead of him letting me pick the smooth in a nor'wester, going out Blossom Pass, he decided to suggest the course. It pushed us right back on the reef-We didn't get hurt, and the boat did not get badly damaged, did not get holed, but it mashed the wood. But we went back out right after that. We waited the five or seven seas for the smooth and went and caught her and hauled her off. Then we pulled her in and went back to get the oars and seats.

I say, and everybody would say the same, that there was never a better boat builder than my father. Sometimes, when he had to caulk his boats, and if he couldn't get caulking, he would get some flour and mix it with paint to make it hard like putty is, and he would fill the seams like that.

Things then were hard to come by. In those days we didn't have any supermarkets, just little bitty stores here and there. We didn't get as much from the United States then, lumber or something like that, but we used to get most of our things from Jamaica. After Jamaica went independent, we stopped trading with those people because after they got their independence, they got out of control.

When we were living there before, they had a few crimes but you could still leave your house open. If the nights were cool, I could walk at night in the country, but not now.

The War broke up everything, stopped everything. My father brought us to settle over in Jamaica. I went out a couple of times fishing in a skiff. My last time out we-my cousin Trilby and I-weren't fishing, we were just rowing and one of those little propeller planes took off. Then it turned and was coming back to the airport. It didn't make it. It got mashed up as we were pulling away. It rocked the boat, it was so close. If we weren't paying attention-We kept off there until the crash boat came out. That was my last time I went out.

During the War, in Jamaica, I missed going out on the water. They had a lot of rules because the War was going on and you couldn't go out. And that knocked it out of us. Later, after that plane, I never did get that feeling back.

Hawksbill Fishing/CINA

Beaching/CINA

North Sound1967/CINAP

CHAPTER FIVE - A Tale

Catboat Courting
by Carolyn Ebanks Watson

Having assured himself that he was a handsome and dashing figure by his brothers' joking exclamations to the opposite, my young Grandpa Lawson took off his jacket, folded it neatly and stowed it aft where it would not get wet. He placed his felt hat atop the jacket and wedged them both with a few sweet potatoes. He would put them on again when they gained George Town dock. His brothers, Timothy and Montgomery, took their places at the pulling thwart, hauled up the mast and pulled up the main sail. They tied off the shrouds and inserted the jib pole over the stem, then hauled up the jib. They played the sheets to let the morning fresh breeze pass by the sails.

At a signal from Lawson they moved to the windward side of the Catboat while he pulled in on the main and jib sheets. The sails pulled power to the boat and off they moved with George Town on the point of the bow a little over seven miles and visible. It was a beautiful morning with a nice breeze from the northeast crossing the boat on its beam. Hardly a flutter of sea to impede their progress.

Timothy and Montgomery chided Lawson in his anxiety at going to see his red-headed Annie Rivers today. 'She is beautiful' is all Lawson could hear, though.

The Catboat moved with a gurgling and creaking of rig from William Barcadere, near Northwest Point in West Bay. They carried sweet potato, yam, pumpkin, pawpaw, saltfish, and a few hens and roosters to sell in George Town. Lawson held his chest out as he steered using the yoke lines. He was in his early twenties then and was proud of who and what he was.

Along the beach, on Boggy Sand Road, Lawson smiled at his friend Abraham riding his white horse with small clouds of sand at his hooves. Lawson steered nearer the shore and exchanged a few joking insults with Abraham. Everybody laughing, he turned the boat back out to cleaner air and scudded toward George Town and Annie.

Red-headed Annie Rivers combed her thick hair over her ears, pulling it to the back into a bun that she held in place with long turtleshell hairpins. She put on her prettiest

George Town, Grand Cayman/CINA

print dress and on her feet, the white keds with the strap over the top that buttoned on the sides. She put on the hat with the pink flowers and went to her mother, who was standing by the caboose heating wash water, to get her final approval. A smile and a steady appraising nodding told her that she was beautiful. But still, her fingers touched imagined pouches under her eyes with a worry. They were caused by not sleeping well that night. She had been so excited at the prospect of the trip to George Town if the weather held, and seeing Mister Lawson. She thought he was the handsomest man in the whole world. He was a turtler and she knew they lived hard lives. The sea, wind and sun made him look older than his years, but they also made him look so mature. He was working hard and saving to build a house, so they would have their own home when they got married.

It was no easy thing to get from Spotts, on the south side of Grand Cayman, to George Town, on the west side of the Island. In those days the roads were nothing more than cow tracks, very narrow and rocky. The only options were walking, horseback, or Catboat, and the boat could only be used when the weather was right. Because of the weather she had not seen him for two Saturdays, and now she could hardly wait. She patted her imaginary eye pouches again gently with fingertips. He would be waiting for her at George Town dock, smiling that smile of his. Hurry up, she heard her father call from the barcadere where he had finished loading the coils of thatch rope into the Catboat and was now getting things stowed properly with the help of her two brothers.

Taking the cushion her mother had made for her courting trips-the boat thwarts made hard sitting-she ran down to the barcadere. Her father took her hand to steady her boarding and she sat on her cushion, placing her hat on her knees. The men pushed the boat away from land with the oars and pulled up the sails. Then, silence. The Catboat moved off with the wind from aft with just enough breeze to cancel the feel of forward motion. It was an easy sail with an easy approach to the dock.

Mister Lawson was there waiting for her. He took her hand in his and helped her ashore. All the men exchanged a few jokes, secured the boat, and Lawson and Annie went up to Mrs. Anderson's house, in the company of her father, to pay a visit. They all sat in the sitting room for a while, sharing the latest news; then Lawson and Annie asked to be excused and went outside to sit alone under the ginnep tree. There they were able to spend some time together and steal an anxious kiss without everyone looking at them.

All too soon it was time for them to go. She left him at the dock, waving until out of sight. He went around to where his brothers were lifting rum glasses at the rum shop.

After a few years of courting in this manner, Lawson Ebanks and Annie Rivers married, moving to their home in West Bay. They had seven children.

Brac Catboat/CINA

... and Songs of the Sea and Catboats
Cayman Islands National Archive

Hawksbill Song
by William Jackson

It was in the month of May

Calbert and Gearman went Bluff Bay.

They caught one hawksbill, so they say,

But old Black Cat went and took it away.

Chorus: Lord, what a misery!

             Wherever I see Bunny,

             People, people will be sorry to see

             The graveyard for Bunny and

             The gallows for me

Aunt Lisha say, "That old Black Cat,

I hope to my God it'll make him fat."

But Tyna say, "I will cut my throat

If Uncle Hedley don't take the case to court."

Chorus-

Coriel, she was sucking bone,

Ina say, "You wouldn't give me none!"

Black Cat break his piece a' spoon,

Digging out that hawksbill backbone.

Chorus-

Gearman say, "If he don't give me some,

I'm gonna drink off Noveela Bay rum,

Then I'm gonna get out on the spree,

And I'm gonna kick old Bunny right in tree."

Chorus repeated twice...

Two Men And A Turtle/CINA

The Turtler's Song

-Anonymous

Down in dear old Cayman

Where the soft winds blow

Out upon the ironshore, though

Mosquitoes bite me night and day,

Cayman girls are sweet of yore

How my heart is yearning to be there once more

Just to hear the boys' gay song.

Breezy Castle mangoes call me back

To the place where I was born,

When the parrot calls I'm lonesome

When a crawl boat comes I'm longing

For some turtle stew.

Makes no difference where I wander

Any place I chance to roam

When I hear the songs I used to sing

Then I'll think of home.

John Howard/CINA

Munzie's Boat

-Anonymous

Munzie boat in the Sound, boys
Munzie boat in the Sound,
When you talking 'bout blue squab head
Blue squab heads all around.

Lambert said to Bertie, "Boy,
Give me a soldier head."
Bertie said to Lambert, "Boy,
All the squabs is dead."

Munzie boat in the Sound, boys
Munzie boat in the Sound,
When you talking 'bout blue squab head
Blue squab heads all around

Munzie said to Lambert, "Boy,
Give me a soldier bait,"
Lambert said to Munzie, "Boy,
All the soldiers are dead."

All the soldiers are dead, boys
All the soldiers are dead.
Bertie said to Lambert, "Boy,
All the soldiers are dead.

North Sound 1967/CINA

Schooners At Regatta/CINA

Goldfield Closehauled/CINA

Breezin' Up/CINA

Off George Town/CINA

North Sound 1967/CINA

North Sound 1967/CINA

Norris Carrying Gerald/CINA

Piggyback, North Side/CINA

Beaching/CINA

Light Airs/CINA *Silhouette/CINA* *Waiting a Breeze/CINA*

Filling Up And Setting Sail/CINA

Blue Light/CINAP

Part Three-To Where and Why
CHAPTER SIX

Restoration of the Traditional Catboat
by Jerris Miller

I was born on the 4th of June in 1956, Gemini, 42 years old.

My father is Ned Miller and my mother is Mary Chisholm Miller. I have two children, Alyssa Michelle and Ned Jerris Miller III. I am married to Catherine Miller. I'm from North Side, more specifically, Grape Tree Point.

My heritage, regarding the Caymanian Catboat, is primarily local fishing and recreation. My best memories of the Catboat, and probably one of the reasons that I am as involved as I am, is because as a kid my uncles would often take me fishing in their Catboats. Easters we did picnics at Round Cay near Cayman Kai, and Catboats were always the mode of transportation. In fact, until I was thirteen, the road to Rum Point stopped right here at our property boundary. Before that you had to walk the beach or sail.

As I grew up, interest in the Catboat died out really, really fast. I would say between the ages of ten and thirty, I had zero contact with the Catboat. There was no operational Catboat that I heard of. Uncle Will's Catboat, that we have rejuvenated, used to sit under a tree all of that time.

Everybody was able to have cars at that time and Catboats went completely out of style. There were three families in Old Man Bay that had Catboats, and one of those, a sixteen-footer belonging to Jim Whittaker, is still functional and in the water. There is another, but they cut and put a motor in the stern of her. Still, she is a twenty-foot Catboat. She belongs to Mr. Whittaker.

Suddenly, at thirty years of age, I really started missing the Catboat. I realised that if an effort was not made to preserve them, my kids would never be sailing them. Now I've got pictures of my kids sailing in our Catboat at the ages of six and three. The pictures are of them in the ocean, behind the reef, out there sailing.

The Catboat went down simply because it was such a utilitarian vehicle for the Island in general and for North

Sailforms On Beach/CINA

Side in particular. As soon as we got roads, bicycles and cars, we lost the need to have our traditional utility vehicle. It was like a pickup truck of days gone by. It was not a necessity any more. It just fell away. Even for fishing it was just a simpler, easier way to go get an aluminum boat with an outboard motor, to do the same things we were doing before.

It is surprising that there just were not a sizeable number of Catboat owners who kept up the maintenance, and to recognise it as an integral part of our history; that we really needed to keep it functioning, to keep it going. But for twenty years, all around the Islands, the Catboat was just laid up on the beach like they were nothing.

The Catboat is an integral part of our history. The design of the Catboat draws very little water; it is a very shallow draft boat. It can float in nine inches to a foot of water because of the way the bilges are built-very wide and low down to the keel. The keel itself extends not much further than six to eight inches. There are unique features to the keel of the Caymanian Catboat because of the uses that it had. This boat had to be able to manoeuvre all around the Islands with a full load, and people really just could not afford to keep repairing them because of the materials involved. You had ironwood in the keel, which allowed it to be dragged over a reef or a sand bar and continue on your way with zero damage to the boat.

Keeping in mind the utility of the boat, the ribs are spaced much closer together than more modern or contemporary boats. It is heavy duty at eighteen inches apart, centre to centre, which translates into a long lasting life and a boat that can take a beating. If you happened to have the boat out there and a nor'wester came washing it ashore, when you got to it, it would not even look like it had been washed ashore when you finished pulling it off. Even the paint they used to use was mixed with a paint oil that had a lot of elasticity and would not scrape off easily.

My theory is that a Caymanian Catboat did not evolve because of the lack of good material that could last. This may sound like a contradiction but because of the materials used, the boat would last for 40 to 50 years. Because of this there was no need to be continually repairing or building new boats. Therefore, the art of building a Catboat was not passed down from generation to generation. The demise came when 50 years later almost all of the boats were in need and there was nobody who really knew how to repair or build them.

Again I will say that until I was thirteen the only way to get from here to Rum Point was to walk the beach or by boat, and if you had a motor you could get outside the reef and you could get there pretty quickly. But in my younger days it was always with a Catboat. It was a beautiful, easy

Catboat Bow Study/Valerie Cottier Photo

Catboat Stern Study/Valerie Cottier Photo

Catboat Port Bow/Valerie Cottier Photo

Catboat Port Stern/Valerie Cottier Photo

reach from here to Rum Point and back up. It was too shallow inside the reef for the motor. The shallow draft of the Catboat developed to give the boat the capability sailing close to shore. As you go around the Island, the breezes are normally perpendicular to the shore, either offshore or onshore. As you go three or four hundred yards off the beach, you will note that that changes and it becomes the prevailing wind of the season, which here is usually from the east. Because of the shallow draft, you could not go to windward very well, but also, if you stay within a hundred yards of shore, you are in a wind pattern that is either coming in or going out, so if you kept close to shore you never had to beat to windward. You could reach right around the whole Island. You could set your sail and never really have to tack and sail right on around to Rum Point.

A lot of my youth I spent watching my uncles come up, after fishenin'-and our grandfather's property has the community barcadere, so a lot of people from North Side brought their boats here and kept them here. The barcadere was donated by my grandfather, William Chisholm. So I saw Catboats coming here throughout my younger years. Mr. Cyril Rankin and Mr. Solomon used to keep their big Catboats here. There was another big one that belonged to Mr. 'Pinkie' Ebanks that was eventually stored on land.

At first a lot of the people cared for the boats. They turned them upside down so no water could collect and rot them, cared for them. But that was my parents' generation, and most of those people have died out. The generation that came after them just threw these things in the yard, and they were burned. First they were used to collect rubbish, and the match was then put to them. Or they weren't turned over, and rot from rainwater and condensation set in. The people who had owned these same boats had had tremendous pride in them, even when they sat on the hard, on the ground. The sad part was, even today; the people who inherited those Catboats would not sell them at any price because of sentimental value. Over the years they have rotted away and been dumped.

Now the next generation, which I consider myself, is coming in and we, for the past several years, have been recognising the Caymanian Catboat as an important part of our heritage. There is now interest, and an effort to bring the boats back. I have personally been working on our boat and the whole concept for the last eighteen years.

Every Cayfest [Cayman Festival of the Arts] for the last six or so years I have delivered our Catboat to take young people out to sail so they can feel the boat in its element. We would put it on the truck and drag her into West Bay, or drag her into South Sound, or wherever they were having the

Grand Cayman Shipbuilding, 1906/CINA

function. We saw it as a chance to expose people to the boat. And always, always there is a huge interest shown by the really older people and the really younger people. It is amazing to see, because there are two generations between those interested, who, I would say, could care less.

I have studied mechanical engineering so I thought at first that I could make a kit from our boat. The kits could be sold for two or three thousand bucks apiece, and at that price you would have fifty Catboats on the Island by today. But building the Catboat is not that easy. They are pretty boats, and from an engineering standpoint the Caymanian Catboat is almost an engineering marvel. Those guys three generations ago were not degreed engineers, and still they developed this by putting one piece in at a time. If you look at the boat front to stern, it is asymmetrical; that is, the bow of the boat is a different shape from the back of the boat. The theory is when you cut the boat up into sixteen sections, the first five-sixths of the boat is fuller than the last sixth.

The theory that I have developed on why the bow sections are fuller than the stern section is so the boat can float over the waves. The bow is fuller so it has more buoyancy and it floats up, but the stern is not. The stern not being buoyant does not force the bow down. The stern is cut thinner so it will essentially sink down into the passing sea, and the boat just seems to mould itself right into the wave, and go over the wave every time. The negative side to this is that many Catboats were known for being swamped from the stern by those same seas.

If you look at the Catboat from the front, there are complex curves to the hull form. Bow to stern, the Catboat is convex and asymmetrical, but keel to gunwale, the boat is concave and convex. So you have two complex curves interacting. When we eventually get this on a computer, it will demonstrate how complicated this is, and even the computer will have a hard time putting this together. The CAD PAC programs I have tried to put the lines on cannot accept the mathematics of the vessel. The Caymanian Catboat is a marvel of engineering. This is the difficulty in making a kit boat. Outside of taking a Catboat apart, it is just too difficult to replicate.

The planking on the Catboat is tapered on the ends in terms of the width, and it is also angled on the edges. Once you get all these angles together on the planks, you have to bend them around these complex curves. Everything will then be parallel. If the planks are cut parallel and you bend them around the complex curves, the edges do not come out fitting. The planking is one-inch thick, what is called five by five-fourths. One-by is usually three-quarter of an inch thick, and five-fourths is actually one inch thick. Eventually, I think it will come down to taking one of these boats apart

Wine Glass/Valerie Cottier Photo

Jerris Miller & Chisholm Catboat/Valerie Cottier Photo

piece by piece and doing the final measurements, and doing the kit from that.

I am aware that with modern materials such as 5200 caulking compound there is a lot more forgiveness, meaning you could fill up a gap. But this is not really what I am trying to do with them. I want to reproduce the boat as it was before. Traditionally, they took those termite hives you see in trees, or mounds you see on the ground, and lit a fire in them, which would last about a week. You collect the ashes and mix them with paint and it makes a perfect putty for caulking.

Replication is the key to reducing the costs. Once replicated, the building of the Caymanian Catboat is just screwing it all together. Anyone can build one. The old people could build one from scratch, but there is hardly anybody left around who can do that now. There are two gentlemen on the Brac, and Ira Walton here. There are no Catboats built-zip-for about a twenty-year period. All of those built in the last seven or eight years were built by Ira Walton. As old as he is, he still works like a young whippersnapper. And even he, since there was a twenty-five year period that he did not build them, is relearning with each one. So the more he does the more he remembers, but also the more he does the older he gets.

To me it is sad that we are losing our data bank in these boat builders.

What I am trying to do is to create a database for one particular Caymanian Catboat. In this case it is a sixteen and a half-foot, fifty-four year old vessel. We have everything for her, even the original sail. That means this sail was sewn up for her thirty-five to thirty-eight years ago. It was the last sail built for this boat, and it was made by Aunt Ida, who runs the Chisholm Store. She still goes to work there every day at eighty-nine years old. She hand-stitched the sail.

I am trying to create an evolution in the construction of the boat rather than an evolution in the construction material of the boat. I feel that if you work in more modern materials, you take away from the real characteristics of the actual boat. It needs to be a heavy boat the way it is. Using newer materials, like fiberglass, means they are not going to rot and are much easier to maintain, but they take away the weight characteristic. The theory there is that we can add the weight to the bottom of the boat, but that will not spread the weight throughout the vessel as it would by using the particular materials that were used. I think it will affect the way the boat rides, and it will certainly affect the way the boat handles.

The method in which all boats were built in Cayman was to take a four- or five-foot piece of Cayman mahogany, and a guy sat down and built a model boat from it. When the full-sized boat was finished, the boat builder would cut the model in half, and that was called a half model. He gave the

Ira Walton Model 'Alsons' for the Fosters/Valerie Cottier Photo

owner half, and he kept half, and that was the blueprint. The half models, to a large extent, have survived, but the techniques of lifting the complex plan from the half model and making it into a hundred-foot schooner has disappeared entirely. This is the reason we need blueprints on paper of as many Catboats as possible, even if they are not functional.

I could use more modern materials and affect the way the Catboat sails to windward. You could put a lot of weight in the middle of the boat, to produce a lower centre of gravity, and it will perform to windward better. But I know that the older people could sail this boat better than I can sail a modern boat. I cannot sail our boat as good as I can a modern boat, but I want it around long enough for me and my children to learn.

There can be a pride available for our interested youth to have in owning something that their grandparents owned. Two generations ago and back, they did derive a lot of pleasure from sailing the Catboat, but by necessity they had to use it. But there is nothing that I like better than to take our Catboat out the channel and

sail with my kids. They enjoy it, and I think back to when my uncles did the same thing with me. There was a difference back then. I mean, they didn't come back in if, as a kid, you got seasick. They came back when they caught enough fish. You were in for a penny, in for a pound.

On the other side, it gives you a sense of accomplishment to go out under sail and catch fish with the Catboat. We know that if everything went to hell, we could feed my family with this boat. And when I am out there, every time I go out, I feel that my uncles are there with me.

Caymanians and a Catboat/CINA

Great Sound/CINA

The Evolution of the Caymanian Catboat

by Carson Ebanks

I will start with an introduction. My name is Carson Kimbal Ebanks. I am 43 years old, married to Susan, and we have four children. I was born in George Town and raised in West Bay. My mother, Ruby Dominguez Hydes, is from West Bay; and my father, Carson S. Ebanks, was born in North Side, his family being from North Side and Little Cayman.

My maternal grandfather, Captain Moses Jacob Hydes, Jr., taught me to sail on Caymanian Catboats. I was twelve, and since that time I have been enthralled by the Catboat of the Cayman Islands. Until the time I went off to University, I used to organise the Catboat races during the old Easter regattas. Up to the age of sixteen, I ventured off into sailing skiffs, canoes, Sunfish® and Dolphin®. Then competition took me on to catamarans, 470s®, Star Boats and now, the J22® and larger keelboats. Competition also took me to three Olympics, the PanAm Games, the 470 Midwinters, the Hobie Cat® Canadian Championships, and the J22 World Championship. Offshore, I raced five Pineapple Cups from Fort Lauderdale to Montego Bay.

I will state unequivocally that there is nothing like sailing the Caymanian Catboat. I am still enthralled at how this boat sails, and I like how it looks.

The demise of the Caymanian Catboat occurred, I believe, because of the technological advancement and economic change brought about by the closure of the turtle industry and the expansion of tourism and the financial industries. Primarily, the Catboat was developed as a workboat associated with turtle fishing. It became less of a viable commercial proposition as turtling fell away. The advent of the outboard motor and the use of fiberglass and aluminum in boat construction also had very important parts to play in the descent of our national vessel.

When I was growing up in the 1960s, some of the larger Catboats were still in existence, but if you combine the outboard motor, the development of fiberglass as a boat-building material with the fact that we were advancing rapidly as a tourist destination, you will see that the results did not prove favourable for our traditional working craft.

Let me elaborate. Previously, there was a great local demand for Catboats to be used for transportation and for fishing. Then, in a relatively rapid transition, roads were being developed, vehicles were being imported and transport changed to motorised modes. On the sea, the tourist industry led to the demand for and development of cabin

Blue Light, North Sound/CINA

cruisers that could easily and comfortably accommodate our visitors. So if you owned a boat, you did not need a Catboat anymore; what you needed was a boat fairly wide of beam, that had an engine, that had cover from the sun, that you could take people around in to either sport fish or on the North Sound to look at the stingrays, dive conch, or snorkel.

The standard size for Catboats was somewhere between sixteen and nineteen feet. I have seen Catboats up to maybe thirty feet. Captain Allie Ebanks, my great-grandfather's half brother, who had captained a famous turtle schooner called the Adams, had five or six of those larger Catboats. They were located somewhere between the Silver Sands Restaurant and the Church of God in West Bay, opposite Captain Allie's house.

The Caymanian Catboat is not an easy boat to build. One difficulty in construction of the traditional boat is that the wood for construction has become less available. You had to go into the bush to cut the timber, and where you could find them was fairly remote and very hard to get to. Normally, the frames are from the plopnut tree that generally grows naturally in the shape of the hull form, and you modify it slightly. Then the main difficulty is in the skill needed to form the planking. Not only are you narrowing the planks toward the stern when you are putting them in place, but you are bending them on different planes as well. You need a steamer to lay out these planks, to make them soft and pliable so that you can mould them to shape.

That shipwright skill these days is used more in fine carpentry or joinery, and those skilled enough find that that calling is rather more lucrative, in terms of remuneration, than building Catboats that nobody is going to use as a recreational watercraft, and even less so as a commercial vessel.

The allure of fiberglass is just that it is very easy to work with and very easy to maintain. If you get a hole punched in it, if you run into a rock or something, you just lay it up and smooth it out, and you would never know you damaged it. Any amateur can fix fiberglass.

So the advent and availability of the outboard motor, the development of fiberglass as a boat-building material, and the evolution of tourism and the financial industries contributed to the demise of the Caymanian Catboat. Our technology changed from a dependency on fishing and turtling, and we did not need the Catboat as a workboat anymore. Without the continuous demand for Catboats, the knowledge of their construction went dormant, and because the construction and learning ceased, the evolution of the Caymanian Catboat halted.

New Catboat with Tiller, Varnished Hull/H.E. Ross

Presently, the whole concept of sailing is getting reintroduced-but it is hard to compete with fast fiberglass runabouts, sportfishing boats and more recently, things like wave runners. It is a hard sell to our youth especially. Young people generally like the excitement of speed, which is not engendered in your typical sailboat.

The Caymanian Catboat is relatively fast, but it will have to continue its evolution to survive. We cannot construct just the traditional Catboat and expect that to maintain any kind of prominence. The method of construction is very tedious and costly; the rig does not seem to be as efficient as a more modern rig with its myriad of sail controls. The maintenance of a traditional wooden Catboat compared to a Catboat built of modern construction materials is likely to be far more costly.

For the New Caymanian Catboat I can foresee changes in sail cloth, in the types of spars, maybe using carbon fibre. I can see the addition of travellers, of downhauls, of Cunninghams, etc. You should have the capability of fine-tuning the New Caymanian Catboat rig.

What we need to aid in the development and evolution of the Catboat is a set of class rules drawn up that would speak to the size, weight and sail area of the New Caymanian Catboat. I personally would like to see some mention of construction materials in these rules. We could then try to get one from each district, with business sponsorship, constructed and racing as a one-design class. Like what happened with Australian dinghies, we could have commercial sponsorship, and we could see what would evolve.

Our heritage and history show community- and family-owned Catboats sailing against each other off the beach, while highlighting their month or holiday. Social gatherings took place on the beach.

Touristically, we could market Caymanian Catboat Regattas as a unique draw. We would have our own indigenous sailing craft racing off the beaches. We could invite visitors to view or participate. Aesthetically, it would act on the whole idyllic perception that you come to a tropical island and you see these serene-looking craft sailing around these beautiful waters. It would add to everyone's image of what the Islands are supposed to be about. All of this would inspire Caymanians to design and construct, using fine boat-building skills, and to revive the Traditional Caymanian Catboat and assist with the evolution of the New Caymanian Catboat.

In this time of progress here in the Cayman Islands, constructing, maintaining and sailing Caymanian Catboats can teach young people (our future) to be self-reliant and to have confidence in their own abilities. It can give a historical perspective on our motto, *"He Hath Founded It Upon The Seas"*, and what type of people they grew from. Our young people would not just have a picture book like this one to look into and say, "Oh, this is what used to happen-"but they could relate it back and say, "Look, we've retained something of the Caymanian way of life. It's still there. You can see it. It is alive."

Regatta/CINA

Pulling Turtle Into A Catboat/CINA

The First Turtle/CINA

Pulling Turtle Into A Catboat/CINA

BIBLIOGRAPHY

The majority of the following reading references were found in the library of the Cayman Islands National Archive, whose ever-improving systems of file and reference are in energetic evolution.

-Ashley, Clifford W.; *The Ashley Book Of Knots*; Doubleday & Co., Inc., Garden City, New York; 1944

- Cayman Islands National Archive & Cayman Free Press; *Traditional Songs From The Cayman Islands*; Our Islands' Past Vol. III;, 1996

-Baker, William A.; *Notes On A Shallop*; American Neptune, 1957

- Burton,Fred & Clifford,Penny; *Wild Trees in the Cayman Islands*; Cayman Islands National Trust

- A. Carr; *Handbook of Turtles*; Cornell University Press, NY, 1952

- Chapelle, Howard I.; The Catboat; *The Catboat Book*; John M. Learens; The Catboat Association with International Marine, 1973, 1991

-Doran, Jr, Edwin Beale.; *A Physical & Cultural Geography of the Cayman Islands*; Doctorate of Philosophy in Geography, Univ. of California, 1949

- David D. Duncan; *Capturing Giant Turtles in the Cayman Islands*; The National Geographic Magazine, National Geographic Society, August 1943

- Hirst, G.S.S.; *Notes on the History of the Cayman Islands*; Benjamin Manufacturing Co., 1910

-Herreshoff, L. Francis; *Sensible Cruising Designs*; International Marine Publishing Co., Camden, Maine; 1973

-Hiscock, Eric; *Cruising Under Sail*; (3rd Edition) International Marine Publishing Company, Camden, Maine, 1988

-Jones, Alick & Sefton, Nancy; *Marine Life of the Caribbean*; MacMillan Education Ltd, 1978

- Jones, Brian; *Geology of the Cayman Islands*; The Cayman Islands: Natural History and Biogeography; Kluwer Academic Publishers, 1994

- Kieran, Brian L.; *The Lawless Caymanas*; 1992

-Marchaj, C.A.; *Sail Performance*; International Marine, Camden Maine; 1990

-Matthiessen, Peter; *Far Tortuga*; 1975; Vintage Books Edition,

-McCarthy, Cormac; *All The Pretty Horses*; Vintage International, Vintage Books, Random House, New York, 1993

-Naylor, Irvin S., Fosdick, Peggy and Sam; Last Chance Lost? Cayman Turtle Farm;, 1994

-Parsons, James J.; The Green Turtle and Man; University of Florida Press Book, 1962

-Pyle, Douglas C. Clean, Sweet Wind; International Marine, 1998

-Rouse, Irving The Tainos; Yale University Press, New Haven & London; 1992

-Smith, Roger Craig The Maritime Heritage of the Cayman Islands: Contributions In Nautical Archeology; A Thesis by Roger Craig Smith; Texas A&M University, 1981

-Street, Donald M.; The Ocean Sailing Yacht; (Volume 2) W.W. Norton & Company, Inc., New York/London, 1978

-Thompson, Ernest F., MSc; PhD; The Fisheries of the Cayman Islands, 1945; on staff at Bingham Oceanographic Laboratory, Yale University

- Webster's Encyclopedic Unabridged Dictionary of the English Language; Portland House, 1989

- Williams, Neville A History of The Cayman Islands; Governor of the Cayman Islands, 1970

- Wood, F.E. & Wood, J. R.; Sea Turtles of the Cayman Islands, Chap.12; The Cayman Islands: Natural History and Biogeography; Kluwer Academic Publishers, 1994

Knob/Clifford Ashley

A GLOSSARY OF TERMS
USED IN THIS BOOK

Apron

- a strengthening piece joining the stem to the keel

Basalt

-an igneous rock formed by a lava flow

Batten

- used in construction it is the line by eye of the curves of the vessel stapled or nailed temporarily in place in a fore and aft position; also light, slender pieces of wood or fiberglass

Bevel

- a gradually sloping angular shaving usually chiseled to allow close fitting of two materials

Boltrope

- a rope sewn along the edge of a sail to strengthen it and take the strain off the material

Boom

- a horizontal spar for extending the foot of the sail

Calabash

- Crescentia cujete, a gourd cut to form like a bowl traditionally used to bail out the Catboat because coincidentally they seem to fit between the timbers perfectly

Caulking

- the cotton or oakum which is driven into a seam to make it watertight

Carbonate

-a salt of carbonic acid

Catboat

- a bow placed single masted sailing vessel with a single fore and aft sail

Cay

- also written Kay, Key, a small island or islet, usually of coral sand as distinguished from a reef islet

Caymanian Catboat

- a single masted, double-ended sailing vessel with a single fore and aft sail that can be propelled efficiently by oar, paddle or pole, utilised for cargo carrying, fishing, turtling, passenger transport or recreation

Cayman Cedar

- Cedrela odorata, a soft wood used in Caymanian Catboat construction of planking, timbers, stem, sternpost, gripe and apron

Cayman Mahogany

- Swietenia mahogoni, a fibrous softwood used in Caymanian Catboat construction of the keel, keelson, stempost, sternpost, gripe, apron, rudder and steering yoke

Cayman Ridge

- a tectonic fault block that uplifts more than 6000 feet above the ocean floor at a 30-degree angle upon which the Cayman Islands are formed. The Ridge stretches from Cuba to the Gulf of Honduras

Brac Catboat/CINA

Cayman Trench

- just off the shores of Grand Cayman the Cayman Trench or Trough is a depression in the earth that reaches a depth of more than 20,000 feet and varies between 60 and 100 miles in width

Clew

-the lower after corner of a fore and aft sail

Coral

-the hard calcareous skeleton of anthozoan animals that can form reefs and islands

Crank

-said of a vessel that is unhandy, easily tipped

Crawl

-also said and written kraal, corral, an enclosure, usually of upright sticks used to keep live turtle until sufficient number to ship

Cuba

- the largest Island in the Caribbean Basin, 200 miles distant and to the North, it is the closest Island neighbor to the Caymans.

Cypress

-Cupressus, an evergreen coniferous tree

Dolostone

-a mineral rock form of calcium magnesium carbonate

Douglas Fir

-Pseudotsuga taxifolia, a western North American conifer

Draft

- the depth of water required to float a vessel

Downwind

-going the direction that the wind goes

Egg bird

-Booby, a sea bird of the genus Sula, related to gannets

False keel

- a longitudinal member added to the bottom of the keel for better stability and windward performance

Fiddlewood

-Petitia domingensis, a fibrous hard wood used in Caymanian Catboat construction of timbers, stem, sternpost, gripe and apron

Foot

- the lower edge of a sail that is attached to the boom

Fore

- toward the bow, forward section, front of the vessel

Fore and aft

- referring to the centerline of the vessel from front to back, or aft

Frame

- a sawn rib or timber, used to form and strengthen the vessel and attach the planks, as well as the backbone pieces

Freeboard

- the height of a vessel's side above the water

Turtle Crawl/CINA

Gaff

-the spar to which the head of a quadrilateral sail is bent or attached

Grand Caymanian Catboat

- the same as a Caymanian Catboat with the exception that it can be fitted with a small bow sprit, mast support rigging and jib, as well as a windward sliding plank called a weatherboard upon which crew members are used as balancing weight

Granodiorite

-a mixture of granite and the igneous rock, diorite

Green Sea Turtle

- Chelonia mydas (reptile), the largest sea turtle and the historic basis for the Caymanian turtle fishing industry

Gripe

- a slender piece of wood that covers the edge of the planks, running parallel to and covering the stempost

Gunwale

- the upper edge of the boat's side

Half-model

- a model of the design of the vessel carved by eye to specification with one half, cut along the midship line, given to the client and one half kept by the builder to serve as a three dimensional blueprint

Halyard

- the rope used for hoisting the sail

Hardwood

- a wood that extremely dense in fibrous compaction, usually very heavy and in the case of some such as iron wood will sink and not float

Hawksbill Turtle

- Eretmochelys imbricata (reptile), the sea turtle most hunted by Cayman Brackers, noted for its shell, which is used in artesan ornamentation

Head

-the top edge of a sail, or the bow of a boat, or the toilet in a vessel

Jib stick

- a cross between a club foot and a bow sprit, it is used mainly on Grand Caymanian Catboats to attach a small jib to increase the windward ability of the Catboat

Keel

- the under laying thick, solid hardwood into which the frames are, and the garboard (first plank from the bottom) is fastened, the stem and sternposts are fore and aft fastened to it to form the backbone of the vessel

Keelson

- the fore and aft member attached atop the keel on which the whole structure of a vessel is built

Leach

- the after edge of a sail

Regatta/CINA

Ironshore/CINA

112

Leg of Mutton rig

- a jib headed rig with the main boom as long as, or longer that the mast and the sail a bit baggy

Limestone

- a rock consisting mainly of calcium carbonate

Luff

- the leading edge of a sail

Lug rig

- a quadrilateral fore and aft sail, the head of which is secured to a yard hung on and projecting a little forward of the mast

Marconi rig

- a triangular fore and aft sail without a gaff or yard, set on the aft side of the mast, also called Bermudian

Mast

-a vertical spar, or stick, used to hoist and maintain up a sail

Master Mariner

-a Captaincy, licensed for all seas, all sizes of ships

Mast hole

-in the Cayman Brac Catboat the hole in the head joining piece in the very bow of the boat, and in the Grand Caymanian Catboat the sailing thwart into which the mast is slid through and stepped beneath

Middle thwart

-rowing stations in the middle of the Catboat

Noddy

-a dark bodied tern

Oar

-a spar used to propel a vessel by pushing or pulling its blade through the water while being loosely attached to the top side of the vessel by oarlocks, tholepins or lashings

Oar (Scull) blade

- the flat part of an oar or paddle

Oar (Scull) loom

- the part of the oar or paddle which one gripes when rowing or paddling

Pepper Cinnamon

- Canella winterana, a light, soft wood used in Caymanian Catboat construction for sculls, oars and paddles

Plank

- the outermost layer of wood in the construction of vessels, laid in horizontal lengths, they can be edge to edge constructed with or without a binding filler called caulking, or laid overlapping called lapstrake

Plopnut

- Thespesia populnea, also called Popnut, a soft but durable wood used in Caymanian Catboat construction of timbers, stem, sternpost, gripe and apron

Paddle, Oar and Yoke/Valerie Cottier Photo　　　　　*Chisholm Catboat Interior/Valerie Cottier Photo*

Pompero

- Hypelate trifoliata, a fairly hard wood used in Caymanian Catboat construction of the keel, keelson, timbers, stempost, sternpost, gripe and apron

Pulling thwart

- the second thwart from the bow, used as a main rowing station, also on Grand Cayman Catboats it is where the mast is stepped

Ranger

-in turtle fishing, a subcontractor to a turtle schooner, who utilises the services of the schooner for a percentage or a fee, while maintaining an independent turtle fishing Catboat

Reef

-a reduction in sail area to counteract too much wind; a ridge of rocks or sand

Rib

- in the Caymans called Timber, the shaped upright internal form upon which the planks are placed, adds strength as a foundation and with the addition of stringers reinforces the form of the vessel

Ripling

- a decorative appearing plank that covers the upper edge of the sheer plank

Rudder

- a fore and aft piece of wood usually attached to the vessel near the stern and in the water that pivots side to side for steerage of the vessel

Sailing thwart

- it is the second thwart from the bow, also the pulling thwart, on a Grand Cayman Catboat and is used to step the mast

Schooner

- a sailing vessel of two or more fore masts and a fore and aft sailing rig, with the fore mast shorter or of equal height to the other mast(s)

Scull

- the Caymanian name for an oar when used with lashings from the top side of a vessel, otherwise an oar used to propel a vessel from the stern top by sweeping in the water

Sea Grape

- Coccoloba uvifera a brittle soft wood used in Caymanian Catboat construction of timbers, stem, sternpost, gripe and apron

Seam

- the space between two planks, or the stitching which holds to clothes together

Shallop

- written also Chaloupe, Shaloop, of European origin it is thought to be the predecessor of the Caymanian Catboat and is described as a single masted, double-ended, undecked boat

Sheer

-the curve of the gunwale or top strake in the vertical plane

All Sails Pulling On The Kirk B/CINA

Sheer plank

- the upper most strake of the topside

Sheet

- a rope by means of which a sail is trimmed, secured either to the clew of the sail or to the boom

Sloop

- descendant from the Shallop, the sloop is a single masted sailing vessel with two or more foe and aft rigged sails

Spanish Elm

- Cordia gerascanthus, a flexible, light, soft wood used in Caymanian Catboat construction for mast, boom and gaff

Spanish Main

- the main lands of South and Central Americas, as well as parts of North America during the times of the Spanish conquest of the New World

Spreaders

- also called crosstrees, they are struts secured on the sides of the mast to give the rigging more spread and thereby more reinforcement

Spruce

-an evergreen conifer of the genus Picea

Steering Yoke

-an athwartship piece of flat wood attached to the rudder head used as a steering bridle with a piece of line on each end

Stempost

- the foremost piece of thick, solid hardwood swooping or standing upright upon which the plankends and the first frames are fastened, fastened fore and aft to the keel to become part of the backbone of the vessel

Sternpost

- the aftermost piece of thick, solid hardwood swooping or standing upright upon which the plank ends and the last frames are fastened, fastened fore and aft to the keel to become part of the backbone of the vessel

Stopwater

- the position where two pieces of wood come together underwater that a hole is drilled in order to allow moisture to escape (to prevent rot) by means of a very soft wood plug

Stringer

- the shape forming batten of a plank used longitudinally inside the frames to hold the shape of the vessel while constructing and reinforce the shape when constructed

Tack

- the lower forward corner of a fore and aft sail, or a point of sailing as close into the direction from which the wind is coming

Taino

-indigenous to the Venezuelan Orinoco river delta, these people under the names Arawak and Ciboney populated the Caribbean Basin prior to the arrival of the Europeans

Template

- An actual size pattern used to draw and cut out parts of vessel to be used in the construction

Tender

- easily heeled or listed, called cranked in the Cayman Islands

Thwart

- an athwartship seat

Trunnel dowel

- originally called tree nails, this cane shaped carved piece of solid wood was used for fastening two pieces of wood together, such as a plank to a frame

Upwind

- into the direction from which the wind comes

Waterline

- the flotation line of the vessel, where it sits on the water

Waterglass

- A box with a glass bottom used to study the sea bottom and search out turtle and fish

Yard stick

- allows for a taller mainsail to be set to rise above and attached to the mast with the halyard block

Using The Waterglass/CINA

LIST OF PLATES AND ILLUSTRATIONS

Regatta/CINA

Derelict In Boatswain's Bay/H.E. Ross

In The Bush/CINA

Drawn Up In The Mangrove/CINA

Ships at Dock, Georgetown, Cayman Islands

Lydia E. Wilson, Nunoca & Admiral Sturdees

Rainbow Discharging Turtle At Kingston/CINA

Three Turtlers/CINA

HE HATH FOUNDED IT UPON THE SEAS